Richard Sennett is one of the most distinguished social thinkers in the world today. His many books include *The Fall of Public Man*, *The Culture of the New Capitalism*, *The Craftsman* and the forthcoming *Building and Dwelling*. Sennett founded the New York Institute for the Humanities at New York University, and chaired a UNESCO commission on urban development and design. In 2006 he served as Chair of the jury of the Venice Biennale. He also chairs Theatrum Mundi, an international network which brings together young architects and planners, with artists working in cities.

Richard Sennett

—

THE FOREIGNER

—

Two Essays on Exile

Notting Hill Editions

Published in 2011
Widworthy Barton, Honiton, Devon EX14 9JS
This edition published in 2017

Designed by by Flok Design Communication GmbH, Berlin, Germany
Typeset by CB editions

Printed and bound
by Memminger MedienCentrum, Memmingen, Germany

Copyright © 2011, 2017 by Richard Sennett

All rights reserved

The right of Richard Sennett to be identified as the author of this work has been asserted in accordance with Section 77 of the Copyright, Designs and Patents Act 1998

This book is sold subject to the condition that it shall not, by way of trade or otherwise, be lent, resold, hired out or otherwise circulated without the publisher's prior consent in any form of binding or cover other than that in which it is published and without a similar condition including this condition being imposed on the subsequent purchaser

A CIP record for this book
is available from the British Library

ISBN 978-1-910749-70-8

www.nottinghilleditions.com

Contents

— Introduction —
vii

— The Jewish Ghetto in Venice —
1

— The Foreigner —
45

— Notes —
97

– Introduction –

I n these two very different essays I've sought to challenge the view that outsiders are hapless victims. Rather than wallowing in suffering, people have to make something of their outsider state, inwardly as well as materially. The Jews of Renaissance Venice who lived in Europe's first modern ghetto sought a new understanding of themselves as Jews, exiled from the home most of them had known over the centuries in Spain. Alexander Herzen, a 19th-century émigré Russian aristocrat forced abroad because of his politics, struggled to understand himself as a permanently unwanted, homeless individual. For both, explicit rejection by a superior force – Church or State – caused them to become foreigners; they had to build a life for themselves in the face of that rejection.

Since I wrote these essays, I've become involved in urban planning work for the United Nations, and so have come into contact with a seemingly very different kind of uprooting. It marks migrants today who flood into the giant cities of the developing world from small villages or farms – tens upon tens of millions of them making this pilgrimage every year in Latin America and Southeast Asia. Sheer poverty, lack of opportunity, or dispossession by giant agribusiness drives them into the city. They are not overtly persecuted as Jews or radicals were in the past; rather, they suffer from indifference, their needs for basic housing, education and jobs neglected by the powers that be.

Yet I often heard echoes of the past in this present reality. Herzen felt the necessity of overcoming homesickness in order to strengthen his will to live – and so too, in the Rio de Janeiro slums, young people with whom United Nations teams have worked speak about not succumbing to regret, as they think many of their parents have when comparing past and present. Sephardic Jews encountered in the Venice Ghetto close up, for the first time, Ashkenazic Jews whose ways seemed utterly alien; the two confessions had to learn how to live together. Similarly, Delhi compresses in the same slums Hindu villagers from very different local religious cultures; to survive together, their sense of 'being' Hindu has had to change.

The word 'foreigner' applies to dispossessed migrants as to persecuted émigrés in the sense that uprooting causes people to become 'foreign' to their customary, familiar selves. As in the case of émigrés, something has to be made of estrangement – it cannot be left as a raw wound; the hapless victim will perish. Making sense of displacement, of one's self-foreignness, is the great inner drama of cities today. For this reason, I hope that the painful work of self-knowledge done by our ancestors will help illuminate the present.

– The Jewish Ghetto in Venice –

EXILES MAKE A HOME

The Jewish people have historically been skilled in the ways of exile. For over three thousand years in Western Europe, Jews survived in small cells mixed among alien, oppressive peoples, a people frequently displaced but sustained in their faith no matter where they lived. They have also created communities wherever they've lived, small, segregated communities, segregation inseparable from their sense of themselves. We tend to think of segregation as power's imposition, which makes of the segregated passive victims. Yet the formation of the Jewish ghetto in Renaissance Venice suggests a more complicated story. It is the story of exiles who were indeed segregated against their will, but who then made new forms of community from their separateness and who acquired an interest, as social actors, in being segregated.

The Jews of Renaissance Venice, and the Jews of Renaissance Rome who followed in their footsteps, gained a certain degree of self-determination in isolated ghettoes. But this segregation increased their Otherness; no longer mixed in urban space, their lives became increasingly enigmatic to the dominant powers beyond the ghetto walls. Fantasies about the

Jews took the place of everyday knowledge about their lives, and those fantasies would in the end overwhelm the ghetto. For the Jews themselves, the ghetto raised the stakes of contact with the outside world: their own Jewishness seemed at risk when they ventured outside ghetto walls. Exposure to others threatened a loss of identity.

This is in a way the story of most groups of displaced persons forced into isolation, but Renaissance Venice made it at once a special story and also something larger: the experience of Jews in the Venetian ghetto traced an enduring way of tying culture and political rights together. Venice was undoubtedly the most international city of the Renaissance, due to its trade; it was the gatepost between Europe and the East, as well as between Europe and Africa – a city largely of foreigners. But unlike ancient Rome, it was not a territorial power; the vast number of foreigners who came and went in Venice were not members of a common empire or nation-state. Moreover, the resident foreigners in the city – Germans, Greeks, Turks, Dalmatians, as well as Jews – were barred from official citizenship in the city. They were permanent immigrants. From this historical frame, among non-citizens, came a conflicting set of codes of rights.

On the one hand, human rights were conceived as placeless: these were rights of contract which applied to all parties, no matter where they came from, where they lived in the city, or who they were. In this, the Venetian right of contract differed from that of contemporary London. In London, the validity of a contract was restricted to people who belonged to the same Commonwealth, which meant geographic, political, and, after the Reformation, religious commonality. In Venice, economic rights operated on a different principle; the very act of contracting was thought to generate rights, whereas rights of contract in Elizabethan England were rights given to the contracting parties by the state.

In one way, the Venetians did tie place to right in the execution of contracts. In Venice, the area around the Rialto bridge developed a set of cultural practices, much like those which later developed in the City of London based on the Venetian example, so that verbal contracts could be effectively binding. For the Venetians, the sanctity of contract derived from rituals of negotiation as well as from the desire of the parties to be trusted in future negotiations; moreover, verbal trust was tied to the use of untaxed or unregistered capital which the parties contracting wished to keep from the eyes of the state, something they achieved by putting as little as possible on paper. These verbal bonds set the sanctity of contract apart from the written law practised in the Doge's Palace in the Piazza San Marco; Venetian law was famous for its elaborate records, its attempt to put everything down on paper – a consequence of its highly bureaucratized state.

The sanctity of verbal contract, I shall argue, established a connection between economic rights and the rights of free speech. Verbal contracts could be revised at any time by the contracting parties, if, for instance, ships were lost at sea or the value of commodities changed on the Rialto. Free speech as a principle was rooted in the desire to make verbal contract a flexible instrument. Economics gave another dimension to the freedom of the word than that annunciated by Milton in the *Areopagitica*, which dealt with free speech in terms of sexual morality and religious heresy.

The creation of ghetto-spaces in Venice, for Jews and for other foreigners, tied place and right together in another way, which can be called rights-in-place. The nature of these rights-in-place concerned protection from violence. The city would protect a Jew or a Turk against Christian mobs at Lent or at other times of high religious passion only if the non-Venetian was in his or her place, shut up in the space reserved for the outsider. Once a person walked somewhere in the city where he or she did not belong, he or she had lost the right to be protected from attack. Place and body were thus concretely joined.

The protections afforded by the ghetto were a new experience for Jews. For the Jews, being 'Jewish' now became spatial experience. The integrity of the human body, guaranteed only in a segregated space reserved for other alien bodies, obviously strengthened the communal bond. More generally, since the high Middle Ages, it had become a commonplace to think of society as a collective body. Segregated spaces like the Venetian ghettoes gave a new meaning to that medieval image. The forces developing modern capitalism detached people from their traditional geographic and social places in society; only those who were officially marginalized were forced to occupy a fixed place. The belief in organic community, a belief held in opposition to the forces of modern capitalism, thus came in more modern times to be embodied by those who were marginal; segregation was made into a positive human value, as though the segregated had been kept from contagion. Ghetto-space was idealized as 'real' community, as an organic space. The Jews of Renaissance Venice were the first to think of their segregation as containing, ironically, this positive virtue.

The governmental apparatus of Venice played a crucial role forming both placeless rights and rights-in-place, since the city-state supervised contracts and policed the city; the city-state acted rigorously to guarantee verbal contracts, even those defrauding the city of taxes. Venice had the most elaborate police force in Europe, and harshly punished informal violence, even for licit ends, as in the murder of an adulterous wife. But in both cases the state structure spoke as though it acted merely as a mechanism, an instrument of economic growth on the one hand, and a regulator of bodily protection on the other. The Commonwealth of Venice, to import the English term, defined itself by the later Renaissance time in terms of civic ceremonial and bureaucratic workings of government itself. The language of placeless rights and rights-in-place drafted by the government was a language spoken about individuals within the city rather than a representation of what the city-state of Venice was itself. In this, the city-state found a certain protection; its own legitimacy was not challenged when either the machinery of economics or the regulation of violence jammed. Polity and city thereby grew apart, in this first 'global city' of the modern world.

The language which gave form to the ghetto of Renaissance Venice, and the construction of rights derived from the making of the ghetto, illuminate current notions of place and right. The dualism which first appeared in Venice was between economic rights of contract and bodily rights vis-à-vis violence. Economic protection was placeless; bodily rights depended upon the body segregated in space. In the modern world the state often makes use of this dualism, to make human rights of unequal value. For oppressed groups, the state is more willing to guarantee the rights of place than universal rights. It will protect vulnerable bodies so long as they stay where they belong, but it gives less protection to the extension of economic power to these bodies in the larger society. Indeed, the state will make use of the values of community to limit economic access to the larger society. Oppressed groups may collude in this limitation on their own freedom, through focusing on the coherence of the community, on the icon of an organic body of the oppressed.

How the Venetian Ghetto was Made

It is easy to imagine today that Jews had always lived in Europe in the isolated conditions of ghetto space. Indeed, from the Lateran Council of 1179 forward Christian Europe had sought to prevent Jews living in the midst of Christians. Rome typified the problem of enforcing the edict of the Lateran Council. Rome had what is now called its ghetto from early medieval times, as did, elsewhere in Europe, cities like Frankfurt; a few streets in the Jewish quarter of Rome could be gated, but the urban fabric in medieval times was too disordered for the medieval Jews to be totally sealed in. Moreover, Jews in most other European cities did not live in tightly packed communities, but rather in dispersed little cells; this was partly a matter of sheer protection, since only through self-effacement and anonymity could they protect themselves from persecution.

In Venice, the physical character of the city, the

fact that it is built on water, made it possible finally to realize the rule prescribed in the Lateran Council. The city's roads are its canals, which separate clusters of buildings into a vast archipelago of islands. In the making of the Jewish ghetto, the city fathers simply put to use the city's island ecology to create a space of segregation. The walls formed by water suggested to Pope Paul IV in Rome in turn how to use walls of stone within the city for segregation; Pope Sixtus V later enlarged and regularized the first Roman ghetto walls. From this walled-in social difference, a new principle in European urban design, ghetto space crystallized as a modern urban form. In the modern world, automobiles and highways take the place of segregating walls.

Why should Venice have had 'a problem' with Jews and other foreigners in the first place? What had drawn them there? The spice trade was a good example of the kind of commerce which had made Venice wealthy, at the price of attracting Jews and other foreigners to the city. The earliest spice which Venice controlled was salt, which provided the most elemental means of preserving food. Venetian salt was dried on the coastal marshes and then sold inland. However, what made Renaissance Venice rich was not trade as embodied by salt, sold according to the old medieval pattern from the city to its immediate surroundings; wealth came rather from trade like that in saffron, for which the immediate local market was small but the European-wide market immense.

By the year 1000, Venice had established itself as the dominant power all around the Adriatic sea, which served as one route to Jerusalem; Venice thus became a crucial city in the European crusades to recover the Holy Lands. By the Third Crusade, the city had acquired trading rights with the East, and these it used to import spices: pepper, some of which came from India, some from the east coast of Africa, via the Egyptian port of Alexandria; saffron and nutmeg from Persia, cinnamon from Ceylon. The Crusaders had returned from the East with the taste of these spices in their memories, and the advent of spices changed the European diet. The trade in spices became so great a part of the Venetian economy that special bureaucracies, such as the Office of Saffron, were set up to regulate the trade.

Wealthy Jews had been coming to Northern Italy from Germany for two centuries before the making of the first ghetto, many of them involved in the process by which profits in foreign goods like spices were turned into investments in diamonds, gold and silver. Jewish banking in the Veneto developed out of the conversion of profits into such assets, which could be quickly resold.

Religious persecution also drove Jews into Venice. Around 1300, pogroms had become severe in Germany, sending Jews to the northern Italian cities of Padua, Verona and Venice. As a result of the wars of the League of Cambrai, in 1509 Jewish moneylenders fled the mainland; about five hundred Jews fled from Padua and Mestre – the terra firma of Venice – to Venice itself. By 1515 the presence of these Jews was felt, however, to be a moral indignity. In Venice in the period from 1510, attacks against them became increasingly shrill. These were led, among others, by the Friar Lovato of Padua, whose oratorical energies in 1511 aroused the Venetians to destroy the homes of Jews living near the Campo San Paolo; two years before he had advocated seizing all the money of the moneylenders, 'and leave them nothing to live on'.[1]

Yet the Jews were not driven away. Economics proved as potent a force as religion. In the words of a leading citizen: 'Jews are even more necessary to a city than bakers are, and especially to this one.'[2] They provided, as well as banking services to traders, loans to the poor and also to the state. Moreover, the Jews could not be expelled without direct cost to the Venetian government: it would lose people who paid high taxes. Out of the conflict between religion and economics came the compromise strategy of spatial segregation in the city, a strategy, in the words of the historian Brian Pullan, for 'the segregation, though not the expulsion, of the Jewish community'.[3]

In the wake of the disasters in the early 1500s

the city began to explore the possibility of using the Ghetto Nuovo as a segregating site. 'Ghetto' originally meant 'foundry' in Italian (from *gettare*, to pour). The Ghetto Vecchio and Ghetto Nuovo were the old foundry districts of Venice, far from the ceremonial centre of the city; their manufacturing functions had shifted by 1500 to the Arsenal. The Ghetto Nuovo was a rhomboid piece of land surrounded on all sides by water; buildings created a wall all around its edges with an open space in the centre. The Ghetto Nuovo was distinctive as an island in the city in that it was connected to the rest of the urban fabric by two bridges only. With these bridges closed, the Ghetto Nuovo could be sealed.

The proposal to make use of the Ghetto Nuovo came from Zacaria Dolfin in 1515. His plan for the segregation of the Jews was this:

> Send all of them to live in the Ghetto Nuovo which is like a castle, and make drawbridges and close it with a wall; they should have only one gate, which would enclose them there and they would stay there, and two boats of the Council of Ten would go and stay there at night, at their expense, for their greater security.[4]

And that is indeed how the Jews lived in the ghetto after 1516. When the drawbridges were opened in the morning, some Jews moved out into the city, mostly around the area of the Rialto where they circulated with the ordinary crowd, and Christians came into the ghetto to borrow money or to sell food and do business. At dusk, all the Jews were obliged to be in the ghetto, the Christians to be out; the drawbridges were raised. Moreover, the windows of the ghetto buildings fronting the exterior were shut every evening, and all balconies removed from them, so that the ghetto wall was like the sheer wall of a castle surrounded by a moat.

This was the first stage of segregating the Jews. The second stage involved expanding the Jewish quarter to the Ghetto Vecchio, the old foundry district. This occurred in 1541. By this time, the Venetians were hurting financially; their customs tariffs had become higher than other cities and they were losing trade. So they decided to lower the barriers a bit, and one result was that Levantine Jews, mostly from what is now Romania and Syria, came to do business in the city. They were slightly more than travelling pedlars and slightly less than bourgeois businessmen; they hawked whatever they could lay their hands on and so, up to 1541, were constantly moving from place to place. The civic worthy Sanuto put crisply the attitude of his fellow Venetians towards Jewish dealers: 'Our countrymen have never wanted Jews to keep shops and to trade in this city, but to buy and sell and go away again.'[5] But now these Jews did not go away; they wanted to stay and were willing to pay a price for it.

To accommodate them, the Old Ghetto was transformed into a Jewish place, its outer walls sealed, its balconies removed. Unlike the first ghetto-space, this second had a small open square and many small streets.

This space of segregation was not the first the city had known. The ghetto took to an extreme the response of Venice to its foreigners which had begun two centuries earlier. It is a response which can be seen applied even to fellow Christians, Germans who were shut up in their own early version of a ghetto, the Fondaco dei Tedeschi – the 'factory of the Germans,' the word 'factory' being used here in the sense of a building in which people lived where they also worked. This combination marked all medieval urban houses. The Fondaco dei Tedeschi was such a house writ large, with the further condition that all its inhabitants were German.

In its early form, the Fondaco was a house of only partial segregation. In principle no one was supposed to leave it after dark, but in fact nighttime proved the busiest part of the day for the Germans, who smuggled goods in and out under cover of darkness to avoid paying customs. In 1479, the government therefore took steps to insure that this place of segregation became a building of isolation; it was decreed that at dusk the windows be shut, and the doors to the Fondaco were locked – from the outside. It was in this year that the house of the Christian Germans became a prototype for the larger urban spaces which would later enclose the Jews.

One other historical frame is needed for the Venetian ghetto, which is its contrast to the Roman ghetto Pope Paul IV began to build in 1555. Paul's ghetto was meant, first of all, to close up all the Jews together in one place so that Christian priests could systemically convert them, house by house, with no possibility of Jews avoiding Christ's word. This translated, in spatial terms, the idea of sheep who had strayed from the flock; kept together, they could be trained. The Roman ghetto was a miserable failure in this, only twenty or so Jews a year out of a population of 4,000 inhabitants succumbing to conversion through spatial concentration. More durably, the Roman ghetto walls cut in two a zone previously controlled by Roman commercial families who traded with the resident community of Jews; in taking over the space of the Roman ghetto for conversion, the Pope also weakened the spatial grip of these Christian families on the city.

The Venetian ghettoes, by contrast, were not meant as spaces for conversion, nor did they lie strategically at the centre of the city. Their geography was marginal to the centre, their land an abandoned industrial site, and the enclosing of the Jewish community in this wasteland aimed at marking the irremediable difference of their being Jewish. But what did it mean to be 'Jewish?' What would living in a space of segregation mean to Jews themselves about their own identity? One way to understand this is by comparing Jews to another marginal group whom the Venetians could not control by spatial segregation. These were the courtesans who formed the upper stratum of prostitution in the city.

Courtesan and Jew

Prostitution may be the world's oldest profession, but in the course of history has taken many forms. In the Renaissance, the courtesan made her appearance as a high-ranking sort of prostitute; she was a young woman who not only sold her body but provided social pleasures for her clients, such as concerts, suppers and private theatricals. The word 'courtesan' came into use in the late 1400s as the feminine form of 'courtier' – in Italian usage, these women were the *cortigiane* who provided pleasure for the *cortigiani*, the men who were the nobles, soldiers, administrators and hangers-on populating the Renaissance courts. The court was a political scene, its dinners, ambassadorial receptions and meetings deadly serious occasions. The courtesan provided men relief from this official world – much as the ancient Greek prostitute was the companion of men at convivial social occasions.

Girls who entered into prostitution of any sort did so at about the age of fourteen. Aretino wrote of a young girl saying 'I learned in a month all that there is to know about prostitution: how to rouse passion, to attract men, to lead them on, and how to plant a lover. How to cry when I wanted to laugh, and how to laugh when I felt like weeping. And how to sell my virginity over and over again.'[6] Becoming a courtesan took longer. It meant establishing a network of highclass clients, learning the gossip of the city and the court to amuse them, and the acquisition of a house and clothes which would be pleasing to them.

Unlike the geisha system in Japan, where the sociable arts were codified into strict rituals taught and passed down from generation to generation, as a lawyer might receive training, the Renaissance prostitute who hoped to become a courtesan had to create herself. In a way, her problem was like that of the male courtier, who had need of such manuals of behavior as Castiglione's *Book of the Courtier*, which told him how to behave in this new institution, the court, which was a power centre unlike the old feudal castle, more cosmopolitan and less bound to tradition than to the shifts of international politics and finance. Castiglione's *Book of the Courtier* told a man how to navigate in a world of strangers. Many scurrilous books purported to give the courtesan similar instruction, but her real education came through learning to imitate upper-class women, to dress, talk and write like them.

In learning 'to pass', the courtesans posed a peculiar problem, one posed also by prostitutes of lesser standing to a lesser degree: if they were successful and learned the art of disguise, they could go anywhere. It was not so much that they could penetrate the spheres of virtuous women as that they could replace them, looking and sounding like virtuous Christian ladies, but also serving as full, erotic companions to their men. It was for this reason that the courtesan was seen as a special threat, the threat of a woman seeming just like any other but sexually free. In a proclamation issued in 1543, the Venetian government declared that prostitutes appear 'in the streets and churches, and elsewhere, so much bejewelled and well-dressed, that very often noble ladies and women citizens, because there is no difference in their attire from that of the above-said women, are confused with them, not only by foreigners, but by the inhabitants of Venice, who are unable to tell the good from the bad . . .'[7]

By Shakespeare's time, Venice had for centuries contained a large cadre of prostitutes who lived off the trade of visiting sailors. Indeed, the sheer volume of money trading hands in the Venetian sex industry during the Renaissance gradually meant that it became 'a legitimate source of profit for noble entrepreneurs of good family'.[8] There were cases of fairly well-born women becoming prostitutes, but they were relatively rare. The more usual pattern of success as a prostitute prevailed: a young girl learned how to pass, and so gained access to more upper-class clients – ships' officers, merchants, members of visiting delegations. In making these contacts some Venetian noblemen assisted them on the quiet for their own profit.

Rome had a rapid eruption of prostitution after the return of the papacy, and as rapid a decline. In 1566 Pope Pius V, in the full flush of the Counter-Reformation, sought to drive all prostitution out of Rome, and, failing in that, to destroy the social standing of the courtesans, in which he was more successful. As long as Venice remained an active port city, it had to tolerate prostitutes as part of its service economy, just as it had to tolerate its Jews who loaned money and changed foreign bills. For any young prostitute, the possibility of becoming a courtesan with such a steady, wealthy clientele was enticing. Faced with this economic reality, the city attempted to treat prostitutes the same way it treated Jews: 'Not only were numerous attempts made to confine [prostitutes] to special quarters, but an abortive attempt was even made on one occasion to require them to wear a yellow item of clothing in order to be clearly recognizable.'[9] Jews in Venice were first required to wear a yellow badge in 1397; prostitutes and pimps were ordered in 1416 to wear yellow scarves. Though it was not required by law, Jewish women seldom left the ghetto wearing any of the ornaments or jewels other respectable women wore. The Jews feared they would provoke resentment if a person in yellow displayed any sign of wealth, so Jewish women, on the few occasions they ventured into the rest of Venice, were remarkable for being plainly dressed as well as dressed with something yellow. The authorities sought to mark out prostitutes in the same way. The decree of 1543, mentioned above, defined those aspects of a virtuous woman's appearance which a prostitute could not adopt: 'Therefore it is proclaimed that no prostitute may wear, nor have on any part of her person, gold, silver, or silk, nor wear necklaces, pearls or jewelled or plain rings, either in their ears or on their hands.'[10] There is a curious irony here, to which we shall return: the virtuous woman may wear all manner of seductive clothing, while the whore must appear plain, as must the Jew.

The dress codes which warned respectable people that they were in the presence of outcasts capped a struggle that had been going on for nearly sixty years to confine prostitutes to a part of the city near the Rialto, again on the model of segregating difference which was carried to an extreme for the Jews. Originally, the Venetians had imagined something like state-run brothels, and purchased two houses for this purpose. But the prostitutes found it more lucrative to work privately through pimps, who recruited clients throughout the city and provided rooms or created anonymous brothels which escaped the state's vigilance; these illegal places for illicit sex could evade the state's proposed taxes, to be carefully calculated on each sexual transaction. The plan for the state-run brothels came to nothing, but the desire to confine prostitutes – who were, after all, offensive to Christian morality – continued, and the 'sex industry' continued to overrun its legal boundaries. Forcing prostitutes and pimps to wear 'Jewish' clothing was therefore the state's second strategy of control, and it again failed, the clothing serving more as an advertisement than as a warning.

By Shakespeare's time, the city was finding it almost impossible to police prostitution by segregation. A law was passed to forbid prostitutes from establishing themselves along the Grand Canal, a position in the city they could afford thanks to their lucrative earning; this only meant they spent their money to infiltrate other respectable areas of the city. By the early 1600s all attempts to regulate how prostitutes looked, so that they could be picked out of a crowd, had also come to grief. The 'Jewish' codes were replaced by edicts forbidding prostitutes to dress using white silk, a fabric meant only for unmarried young ladies and certain kinds of nuns, or against adorning their hands with the rings of married women. All were useless: the state could no longer control sex in the city.

Why should ghetto-ization work for some kinds of differences in the city but not for others? Why, in the case of Venice, should religious and ethnic outsiders be controllable by isolation but not sexual outsiders?

The courtesans had no interest, economic or personal, in being so isolated, and so they resisted with every means at their disposal. The Jews, on the other hand, faced a more complicated reality. They protested against the severity of this form of isolation yet also participated with the authorities in negotiating the terms under which they would live in a ghetto. They did not enter the ghetto passively. In exchange for segregated isolation, the Jews gained their bodily security within the walls of the ghetto, so long as they stayed there. This guarantee was made by the physical space itself. The isolated space protected them in 1534, for example, when the Jews were subject to a wave of attacks during Lent; the bridges were drawn up, the windows closed, and the crowds of Christian zealots couldn't get at them. In its dealings with all the foreign communities, the city-state was willing to prosecute violent crimes so long as the foreigners were in their own quarters; it abjured, in practice, prosecuting violent attacks on foreigners outside those quarters.

Secondly, while the state had nothing to offer the

courtesan in exchange for wearing the yellow scarf, it did have something positive to offer the Jew for wearing the yellow badge. In exchange for the Jews entering the ghetto, the state allowed them to build synagogues. The synagogue, which in the Middle Ages consisted of a congregation meeting in a home or in a nondescript building, was in the ghetto protected by a Christian state. The synagogue building became the defining public institution within the life of the community, and the ghetto soon became the site for synagogues representing different confessional groups – Sephardim, Ashkenazi, even a Chinese synagogue for the nineteen Chinese Jews living in Venice in the mid-sixteenth century.

This concentration of different kinds of synagogues in the urban ghetto had a profound effect on the very concept of Jewish identity. The strands of Renaissance Judaism were woven of very different social materials. Ashkenazi Jews did not speak the same language of Sephardic Jews, nor share a common culture, and the doctrinal differences between them were great. Levantine Jews composed Jews of several schismatic sects whose language and customs and economic activity bore little resemblance to those of Western Europe; the condition of a Chinese Jew is in turn almost impossible to imagine joined to that of other Jews. Yet joined they were, all constrained to life in the same dense, bounded space, and this re-enforced the single characteristic they shared, that of 'being Jewish'.

The forging of this identity appeared in quite concrete ways; the different kinds of Jews co-operated to protect their interests, and evolved forms of collective representation so that they spoke as 'Jews' to the outside world. In the Venetian ghetto, as shortly afterward in the Roman ghetto, the Jews formed fraternal organizations, which met in the synagogues but which dealt with purely secular matters concerning the ghetto. Since they were meant to live in isolation, much of this secular work was aimed at self-help in coping with the physical conditions of the ghetto itself.

The growing population of the ghetto gradually made this enclosed space a place of filth and disease; plague found a welcome home here. The Jews sought to protect themselves by recourse to their own doctors, for medicine was the one liberal profession which they were allowed to practise in the city. But working against medical knowledge, even in its primitive form, was the law of housing to which the Jews were subject: they were not allowed to own the buildings of the ghetto, but were permitted only to build higher the existing houses and internally to divide the buildings up into ever smaller apartments. The work of the Jewish fraternities controlled the space of the ghetto, but it was a physically putrefying space.

In Venice, the economy built on spices had a

profound effect on the religious life of the ghetto, measured in terms of coffee. Traditionally, ordinary Jewish prayers and religious study in the late Middle Ages occurred in the morning. The advent of coffee, readily available in the city, was greeted by the Jews as a way to make use of their spatial segregation. They used it as a stimulus to stay up at night, the hours of prayer and study now being the hours in which they were incarcerated at night.[11]

By such means, by their very enclosure within ghetto-space, the Jews, like Venetian Germans, Turks and Greeks, felt a sense of solidarity with one another; in isolation these aliens 'constructed' the sense of a collective character. By contrast, it would have been meaningless for prostitutes to forge solidarity in that form; there was no nation, no memory, no anthropology from which prostitutes could make of themselves a people.

The space of Jewish identity was connected to the body in other ways, connected via the way Jews made money, through usury. As practised in Venice from the twelfth century on, usury consisted in lending money at rates from 15 to 20 per cent, which was less on the whole than rates charged in more northerly countries. Wherever it was charged, and by whomever, it was thought Jewish money, since it was considered an unclean form of wealth. In the *Nicomachean Ethics*, Aristotle had condemned usury as a 'gain of money out of itself', as though money could breed like an animal,[12] and this 'unnatural' connection to money was offensive. (A 'clean' Venetian loan in this early moment in capitalism meant a low, variable rate of interest, and no security on which the lender in fact collected.) As an unnatural practice, usury was compared to illicit sex: a contemporary of Shakespeare's declared, in *The Seven Deadly Sins of London*, that 'The usurer lives by the lechery of money, and is bawd to his own bags'; another Christian critic of the Jews wrote that the usurer 'puts his money to the unnatural act of generation'.[13] Elsewhere, the money gained through usury was compared to excrement, and the Jew compared to a coprophage.

From pre-Hellenic times, Judaism itself had been concerned with rituals of the purification of the body. The *Mikvah* baths for women were such a ritual, as was the cleaning of the house to inaugurate important religious festivals. In the medieval era, Jews began to survive economically by practices which made them seem unclean to others, and now that issue of bodily cleanliness, encoded in religion from within, inscribed by social prejudice from without, could be addressed in the ghetto in a new way. Spatial separation could be made into a virtue, removing the community from the taint of pollution. The struggle against plague, itself compounded by the ghetto-space, took on a religious character. It gave a new, visual dimension to the fundamental

Hebrew word '*Qadosh*'. As Kenneth Stow remarks, *Qadosh* 'literally means separate or separated. This is its original, biblical sense. The link with godliness is in Leviticus: "You shall be Qedoshim, for I, the Lord, your God, am Qadosh."'[14] Spatially segregated, they began to conceive of the ghetto as setting themselves a new task, the task of purification, purification of the community by making use of its separation. But how could this task co-exist with their economic lives outside the ghetto, and the margins of social exchange with Christians which co-existed with their own marginality? How could a life in the ghetto be yet an urban life? These questions shaped the issue of rights.

Two Ghetto Lives

The plot of Shakespeare's *The Merchant of Venice* turns on a circumstance which seems odd the moment we think about it. Shylock, the rich Jewish moneylender of Venice, has lent Bassanio three thousand ducats for three months, and Bassanio's friend Antonio has pledged to repay the loan to Shylock. If Antonio fails, Shylock, who hates the aristocratic Christian Antonio and all he stands for, wants a pound of Antonio's flesh as a forfeit. Fortune goes against Antonio; ships carrying all his wealth are ruined in a storm. Shylock then wants his pound of flesh.

The odd thing is that neither Antonio, nor the Christian authorities who now enter the action of the play, should feel obliged to keep their word to a Jew. The economic system, as we remarked, made great use of verbal contracts; written records were kept but the crucial matter was one's word as one's bond. In the banking system at the Rialto, as described by the historian Frederick Lane, transfer payments occurred as follows: 'the banker . . . sat behind a bench under the portico of a church at the Rialto, with his big journal spread out in front. The payor orally instructed the banker to make a transfer to the account of the person being paid.'[15] The Rialto, the centre of economic activity, filled up every day with gossip and news; capitalism was practised without statistics or government guarantees of any sort; trust in the character of others was crucial to doing business with them.

Outside the theatre, Shakespeare's audience in England, like Sanuto in Venice a century before, treated Jews as half-human animals, incapable of being trusted. In the play, Shakespeare compounds these prejudices by making the Jewish moneylender into an effective cannibal: Shylock proposes to carve a pound of flesh out of Antonio's hip if the nobleman cannot pay up. The unnatural practice of usury is taken to its most inhuman bodily conclusion.

Thus, the audience should, it would seem, expect the Duke (the Doge) of Venice to enter, a powerful *deus ex machina*, and throw the cannibal into prison, or at least declare the contract immoral and therefore void. Yet when one of the minor characters in *The Merchant of Venice* says he is sure the Duke is going to solve things exactly in this way, Antonio responds

> The Duke cannot deny the course of law,

and explains why in terms of how the city flourishes:

> For the commodity that strangers have
> With us in Venice, if it be denied,
> Will much impeach the justice of the state,
> Since that the trade and profit of the city
> Consisteth of all nations.[16]

In giving the Duke these words, Shakespeare makes an argument to his audience which explained to them something about their own lives, rather than characterizing their relations with the tiny population of Jews among them. Wealth in the city requires people to accept moral impurities. Shakespeare's Duke goes even further: for the sake of 'commodity' – ease of commerce – people must honour contracts, no matter what one thinks of the moral qualities of the parties to them, or indeed the morality defined by them. Even cannibalism has to be tolerated, if both parties agree to it and it concerns only themselves. In this way, contract appeared as a force which generated its own rights, claims and entitlements; no higher law, no outside rule, can intervene in its workings.

The cannibal contract between Shylock and Antonio is a verbal contract, and it is its verbal qualities that Shakespeare has the Duke address, when he confronts Shylock. The Duke reasons with Shylock, rather than orders him to desist; if the contract is to be broken, it can only be done so by the process of people speaking to one another. Shylock can in turn mock and insult these Ducal pleadings because he knows he is 'within his rights' to say whatever he wants. This is what Portia, the woman who will eventually cut this Gordian knot, means when she declares 'There is no power in Venice can alter a decree established.'[17] The 'decree' is the agreement which both Antonio and Shylock entered into through verbal negotiation, and Shylock's freedom of speaking to the Duke, insultingly, combatively, derives from the same source – the legitimation and protection of words in themselves. The action of the play thus dramatizes a connection which began to take form in the Renaissance: the connection between freedom of speech and the sanctity of contract. This economic freedom derives from freedom of speech.

Since Shakespeare is a dramatist, the freedom to speak which he discovers in this cannibal contracting serves an artistic purpose; it is to deepen the stereotypical image of the greedy Jew. In this, *The Merchant of Venice* marks a sharp contrast to Christopher Marlowe's play *The Jew of Malta*. Marlowe makes Barabas, the Maltese Jew, into a figure of fun, and merely contemptible because of his greed. Shylock is a more complex human being, his greed intermixed with rage against the Christians who deny him the elemental consideration due to another human being. The most famous speech by Shylock is an attempt to restore the dignity of the body to Jews: 'Hath not a Jew eyes? Hath not a Jew hands, organs, dimensions . . . If you poison us do we not die? And if you wrong us shall we not revenge?'[18] The speech appeals to the universality of the body, to all bodies having equal rights, including the right of revenge. And in turn, Shylock's appeal frames the denouement in the following fourth act, when Shylock's contract is finally defeated by Portia.

In *The Merchant of Venice*, Shakespeare surprises us at the denouement. He has built up a great drama of right versus morality; suddenly, in Act IV, he dissipates its tensions. Portia, in disguise as a lawyer, tells Shylock his claim is just, but that he must absolutely adhere to its terms, taking a pound of flesh but not a drop of blood, which was not specified in the contract; moreover, he can only carve a pound of flesh, not an ounce more or less. Since Shylock cannot be so scientific a cannibal, the game is up. Many critics have found this a lame conclusion; the larger conflict seems evaded by a kind of lawyer's trickiness. Yet it accords well with the entire thrust of the play: the powers at work in Shakespeare's Venice are powers which detach people from the texture of circumstance, the burdens of place.

Those powers of detachment from circumstance and place are nowhere in the play made more evident than in the figure of Shylock's daughter Jessica. The moment she falls in love with a Christian, Jessica flees her father, her house, and her faith. She evinces remarkably little grief at leaving the world of her father – nor at robbing him, which she does when she takes jewels from Frankfurt to pay for her own pleasures on her honeymoon. Recounted thus, she seems a vile creature, yet in the play she is wholely charming. The reason for this is that Shakespeare doesn't imagine 'Jewishness' as racial curse, or racial at all, or even a cultural identity. The weight of 'being Jewish' is indeed light in *The Merchant of Venice*; 'being Jewish' is here rather like wearing a set of clothes, which you shed if you happen, for instance, to fall in love.

The contractual trickiness Portia practises on Shylock conveys the same weightlessness. This, as I read it, is the ethical insight Shakespeare had into the rights of contracting: in freeing men and women from the force of circumstance, the work of words robs them of the density of experience as well. Action, such as Portia's lawyerliness, and character, such as Jessica's Jewishness, both become weightless under the work of words; Shylock's mortal rage is dismissed, both his evil and the nobility of his great speech about the Jew's body forgotten; his daughter has robbed him and left him. All this is hardly a Christian resolution of events; Shakespeare called *The Merchant of Venice* a comedy with reason, since good and evil end in inconsequence. It is a commonplace to call *The Merchant of Venice* a play about exchange, but the subtext of exchange in this comedy is indifference.

As modern readers we know the social reality of indifference contained in the ethos of the sanctity of contracts. The disturbance to a modern reader, minded of human rights, is the connections made in this drama between the sanctity of contract and freedom of speech. This was the emblem of Venice to Shakespeare and his contemporaries – the emblem of a place of wealth gained, in their eyes, by new and modern means, an international city cut loose from localism, Europe, and the power of Christian rule. This vision of a city cut free from old cultural bonds is of course not the Venice of the Jewish ghettoes, or the Fondaci of the Germans, Turks or Albanians. If *The Merchant of Venice* can be read, as I think it can, as one kind of premonition about modernity, about the experientally eviscerated meaning of freedom in the modern world, the ghetto of Venice offers another premonition.

Leon (Judah Aryeh) Modena, who lived from 1571 to 1648, spent most of his adult life in the Venetian ghetto. He was a scribe, a poet, a rabbi, a musician, a political leader, a scholar of Latin, Greek, French, English, and, surprisingly to us, a compulsive gambler; his autobiography's title *The Life of Judah* is a play on words, since gambling was supposed to be the sin of Judah.

Born outside the city, Modena came to Venice in 1590, when he was nineteen years old; three years later, now married, he decided to become a rabbi. It took him nearly twenty years to achieve this aim; he was thirty-eight. His life in those twenty years was unsettled; he wrote a great deal, travelling from place to place, but felt uncomfortable. The quintessential Wandering Jew, it was only when he entered the closed world of the Venetian ghetto, surrounded by Jews of every sort leading an active public life, that he began to feel truly at home.

When in 1609 he was finally ordained in Venice, his life took on an intensely local character. A rabbi in Renaissance Venice attended the synagogue three times a day 'to lead the service, to recite prayers for the sick and the dead, to preach every Sabbath morning before the Torah was removed from the ark to be read, and to teach two or three laws after it was read and returned to the ark Mondays and Thursdays'.[19] Because of his intellectual gifts and his ceaseless writing, his sermons became internationally famous, and he began to attract many Christians into the ghetto to hear him speak.

Leon Modena was the foremost, but not the first, rabbi to attract Christians. As the synagogues took shape as public institutions – buildings separated from the twisted interiors of Jewish life, fronting the south-east corner of the Ghetto Nuovo and the main street of the Ghetto Vecchio, buildings which could be easily found and entered – they became places within the ghetto where, occasionally during the daytime, the cultural distance between Jews and Christians were breached. Given a sufficiently eloquent speaker, Christians would come, albeit infrequently, into the ghetto to hear him talk in the synagogue. Rather like modern European tourists going to Harlem, these ghetto visits were usually a matter of voyeurism. Christians like Paulo Scarpi, who came to listen seriously to Modena, paid a penalty; for Scarpi, it meant being denied a bishopric because he had 'consorted with Jews'.

Modena's personal gifts constituted a kind of test case as to how far an illustrious man could break the isolation of the ghetto. Throughout the 1620s his reputation rose, to a summit in 1628 when he took control of the Jewish musical academy (l'Accademia del' Impediti) and gave performances of Jewish choral music and Psalms in the Sephardic synagogue. 'The Christian nobility of Venice flocked to this spectacular event,' in the words of his most recent biographer, 'and the authorities had to intervene to control the crowds.'[20]

Modena, as the modern historian Natalie Davis points out, 'is discrepant from Shylock on almost every page: a Jew who chances his money with thriftless abandon, . . . who basks in Christian admiration . . .'[21] And yet as his life drew to its close, the very conditions of the ghetto which made it possible for him to flourish – its formal establishment within a city, its magnetic attraction to Jews who wandered elsewhere – closed in upon Leon Modena.

When a great plague swept through Venice from 1629 to 1631, the segregation of the ghetto that barred Jews moving out to other more hygienic places meant that those under Modena's pastoral care suffered particularly from the ravages of the disease. Three years later, in 1634, Modena's grandson, all of fourteen, thought the great fame of Leon Modena would earn him his own liberty as a printer, but that fame proved to have personal limits, and the boy was thrown into jail. Modena himself found the limits of his regard in the eyes of Christians; for the publication of his magnum opus on Jewish religious rites he was hauled before the Venetian Inquisition in 1637, and only his personal relations with the Grand Inquisitor saved him and his book, which continued to be excoriated by lesser dignitaries of the Church. Modena's book on Jewish ritual was a threat to the Inquisition because it placed in the overt, public realm of anthropology what had before been confined to the shadows as fantasy. Above all, in these years as his life drew to a close, he was to discover the terrible connection between psychosocial fantasy and spatial segregation.

In March of 1636, goods stolen elsewhere in Venice were received and hidden by a group of Jews in the ghetto. Modena describes how the police organized the search for hidden silk, silk clothing and gold. 'On Purim the ghetto compound was closed off in order to conduct a house-to-house search in great haste.'[22] Because of the way the space was organized, this could be done simply by drawing up a few bridges and locking a few doors. Modena railed against this, saying that 'when one individual committed a crime, they [Christians] would grow angry at the entire community . . .' But then he writes a revealing conclusion to this sentence: 'calling us a band of thieves and saying that every kind of crime is concealed in the ghetto.'[23]

By the time Shakespeare wrote *The Merchant of Venice* the Jews of the city had become indeed enigmas to their Christian contemporaries, who no longer saw Jews routinely in their midst, save on those few occasions when Modena himself had attracted them into the ghetto. Rumour flourished unchecked about how the Jews lived. In part this was simply because an ever larger number of Jews were coming into the city and then disappearing into the ghetto. But by shutting away those who were different, the larger society could know about those who were segregated only through fantasizing about them. In 1636, the fantasy that all Jews were engaged in a stolen-goods ring became, in the course of two or three days, an unshakable conviction in the minds of the Venetian public. Since there was no daily fraternizing with most Jews, there was no experience to limit the play of fantasy. From the stealing, other crimes were devised in the minds of those beyond the ghetto's walls, such as the imprisonment of Christian children in the ghetto, and the practice of Black Mass. The ghetto had become in the eyes of the Christians a space of concealment; behind its drawn bridges, its closed windows, its life shut off from the sun and the water, crime and idolatry were thought to fester precisely because this was a life which could not be casually, easily *seen*.

As rumour mounted in the next few days, Jews suffered the largest pogrom known in Europe since the Roman emperor Hadrian had made war on the Jews of Jerusalem fifteen hundred years before. The Venetians had concealed difference, and in a pogrom like that of 1636 – for such it was – the Jews now lived out the consequences of the policy of isolation. In a ghetto-space perceived from the outside, fantasy converts difference into an incomprehensible Otherness.

And so the rights-in-place that the Jews had

enjoyed broke down. The state apparatus could not protect their bodies, because popular passion, mobilized by fantasy, proved stronger than the state's police powers. There is debate among historians about the degree to which the police were themselves part of the mob, but the result of massing so many Jews together, making the community so coherent in space, was that, once the gates were breached, the Jews could be attacked like animals penned up for slaughter.

In the Venetian ghetto, Modena the Wandering Jew, the cosmopolite par excellence, had at last become Jewish, his faith coterminous with his space. In the wake of the pogrom of 1636, he began to rue the life he had settled into. His son-in-law Jacob, with whom he was very close, had been banished to Ferrara as part of the general punishment inflicted on the Jews in the persecution of 1636. Now in 1643, ill, persecuted by his own wife, lonely, Leon Modena asked the authorities to let Jacob return. They refused, still reeling under the fears which had caused the great persecution. Modena then succumbed to a severe bout of his life-long vice, 'playing games of chance. I persisted in this [for two months] at great monetary loss, as well as much loss of honor, the likes of which I had never experienced before, and quarreling at home, too.'[24] All his life he had gambled not for pleasure but in desperation, when his own efforts seemed incapable of guaranteeing his survival.

The elderly rabbi and world-renowned scholar now seated himself at the gaming table, rolling dice and drawing cards week after week, as though the sheer rituals of betting might ease his pain.

The memoir near its end bursts out with a terrible confession of helplessness: 'Who will give me learned words of lamentations, moaning, and woe so that I may speak and write of how much worse my luck has been than that of any other person? I shall suffer and bear what began to make me desolate on the day I was born and has continued without respite for seventy-six whole years.'[25]

A great irony of urban form is the ghetto-spaces Venice made for its Jews, Germans, Persians, Greeks, and sought to make for its courtesans. Looking strictly at its population, we would say that Venice was the most diversely provisioned city in Renaissance Europe; no other city contained such a cosmopolitan population. The economic conditions which created the wealth of Renaissance Venice provisioned the city abundantly with human beings, but that very abundance was shunned as daily experience by this city of material luxury. One conclusion would be that here is cause and effect; society could not support the diversity brought into the city by the economy – an argument heard frequently today in mixed cities like New York, Berlin or London. What weighs against this argument is that the ghetto is not something that happens *to* the Jews, as passive victims. Through their confraternities which mediated relations with the outside world, in the gradual identification of faith with space, they became men and women of the ghetto, a space at once of repression and a space of identification.

It could be said that the Jews of Venice had no choice, but this evades the issue. Jews who refused this way of life left the city. The dichotomy which marked the modern history of the Jews began in the possibility of living territorially, under the conditions imposed in Renaissance Venice and Rome. Those Jews who rebelled against ghetto-ization suffered uprooted lives; those Jews who accepted ghetto-ization suffered from their very rootedness. At the end of his days what Leon Modena came to see was that this rooted space was in its own way disempowering; right-in-place was overwhelmed, overwhelmed by the spatial illogic of Otherness.

Conclusion

I have not tried, in this brief sketch, to write an innocent history. The story of the Jews in Renaissance Venice, and the differing concepts of rights associated with their presence in the city, has seemed to me to bear on current thinking about human rights. In the last few years, discussions of rights have been oriented to civil society, that is, to religious, economic and communal practices. This discussion has sought to provide an understanding of human rights as themselves social practices, practices which transcend legal formulations and the hegemony of the state. Few modern thinkers would follow Hannah Arendt to the bitter end, in her divorce of politics from the sphere of civil society; nonetheless, there is a tendency to accept the distinction she makes, but from the other side, so that the realm of social practices appears as a corrective to legal formulation of rights.

The history of the Venetian Jews, as I have recounted it, might give pause to those disposed to this corrective view. For it is a history in which the discursive powers of human beings, and the spatial organization of human lives, both vitiate the very experience of entitlement. The cultural formulations of rights in speech and in space can prove illusory or self-destructive. The state is, in my view, a necessary corrective to the norms of right within civil society.

I have focused in this essay on the relation of place to right for a further reason. The ideology of place – in the form of celebrations of the local, or in the form of ideals of a common culture among a particular group – is today set against the universalizing claims of the Enlightenment. The illusion of Enlightenment thinkers like Kant was that the social could be comprehended within the political;

this illusion is countered today by a celebration of social cohesion in and for itself, especially among oppressed groups. That effective rights can be generated by the sheer act of social cohesion seems to me as grave an error as Kant's notion of universal citizenship proved to be.

The placeless claims of contract, such as appeared in Venetian capitalism, were flawed because of the very mobility of the spoken word. The struggle to achieve specificity in written law seems to me the only way to counteract this verbal 'lightness of being', to adapt a phrase of Kundera's. The Venetian Jews possessed both verbal and spatial rights which nonetheless did not incorporate them into the codified workings of the state. Theirs were rights of toleration, rather than rights of legitimation. In my view, only the state can do that work of legitimation, and can do so only by rescuing words from the realm of spoken understandings.

– The Foreigner –

Manet's Mirror

Edouard Manet was a painter of the city but no realist, as we commonly understand that term. He did not seek to achieve in painting the effect of surprising life in the raw, as did photographers of his time. Nor did Manet's record of Paris share much in spirit with Zola's declarative, indignant literary portraits of the city's whores, abandoned children, or families dining on roasted rats. Manet's art is capable of stunning direct political statement, as witness the painting he made in 1868, *The Execution of the Emperor Maximilian*, but the artist's vision of the city relies upon other means for its effects.

In recording the life he saw in Paris Manet made use of visual gestures which trouble the eye, which wrench it from object to object within the frame of the painting, and which often suggest that the real story of the painting is happening elsewhere, off the canvas. In painting the city, Manet is an artist of displacements. It is in his understanding of displacement that the artist speaks to us socially, today as in his own time; his art challenges certain assumptions we may make in describing people who are displaced economically or politically: the immigrant, the exile, the expatriate.

These words name the differing reasons a person may live abroad, but the result of such displacements seems, today, a fate in common. To be a foreigner is to live ill at ease abroad – the immigrant who is culture-shocked and clings to his or her own, the exile who hibernates indifferently in a city barely touched, the ex-patriot who soon dreams of returning . . . Such images sentimentalize the need for roots and the virtues of the hearth. More, they deny to those who become foreigners the will and capacity to make something humane from the very experience of displacement, even if forced initially to migrate. A painter completely at ease in his city, interested in the smells and shadows of its everyday life, Manet yet imagines what is positive about the very experience of displacement. The duality of 'home' and 'foreign' comes apart under his brush, since the imagery of familiar places becomes itself increasingly strange and foreign.

Manet's eye for displacement is given full rein in his last major work, *The Bar at the Folies-Bergère*, painted over the winter of 1881–2. The painting has an interesting history. In 1879 Manet proposed himself to the Municipal Council of Paris as the painter of murals for the new Hotel de Ville; these murals of modern Paris would show the effect on the life of the city of new constructions – the steel bridges, the poured-cement sewers, the wrought-iron buildings. Manet's proposal was rebuffed, and it is significant that this, the great work he turned to after his denial, does not present one of the scenes envisioned for his murals of Paris, but rather turns to something seemingly more sentimental, more kitsch even, a picture of the Folies-Bergère. What Manet would seek to do is infuse this banal scene with the force of all the changes he felt at work in Paris, changes which had spurred the development of a modern sensibility.

It is important for us to understand, in retrospect, what the Folies-Bergère of Manet's time was, and was not. It was a place of sensual license: both female and male prostitutes drifted among its crowds, and there were performances of the cancan, which in its nineteenth-century version was nothing like its more modern, sanitized descendant (the cancan, introduced into Paris in the 1830s, was usually danced by women with no underclothing beneath their loose, short skirts, so that every time they kicked their legs their mounts of Venus were disclosed to view). The Folies-Bergère was not itself, however, a whorehouse, though conveniently located to several, a fact which meant that it was possible for women to frequent it for amusement – which surprisingly respectable women in surprisingly respectable numbers did. This, then, is a risqué place but a public one, filled with noisy crowds drinking and flirting, the air perfumed by cigars, coffee and cheap Beaujolais. Parisians went to the Folies when they wanted to relax. It was comfortable and homey, a home away from, very far away from, the rigours of the family home.

Such is the scene Manet will take apart. We are shown a woman standing behind a bar: pensive, sad, unsmiling, an isolated figure in the midst of noise (the painted figure is based on Suzon, a barmaid at the Folies-Bergère whom Manet knew). The viewer is drawn into this scene though the use Manet makes of mirrors, mirrors which create a special experience of displacement.

The barmaid is painted so that she stares directly out at the viewer. The mirror in front of which she stands is also directly opposite the viewer; Manet reinforces this full-frontal alignment by how he places the barmaid's arms and hands on the bar: her arms are extended and her hands are turned out, as a ballet dancer would turn out the legs in the fullfrontal 'address' of the body. Directly to the right of this figure we see her back reflected in the mirror, the flat mass of her black dress exactly the size of the body, so that the reflected figure lacks perspectival diminishment; the reflection seems in the same dimensional plane as the body. I say we see her reflection in a mirror, although optically this is impossible; we could not be facing her directly and seeing her reflection to the right of her at the same time. Today the viewer accepts this impossibility; it seems visually logical if optically impossible. However, Charles de Feir, in his *Guide du Salon de Paris 1882*, spoke for many of Manet's contemporaries in finding this strange mirror a sign of the painter's faulty technique.[1]

In many of Manet's late paintings, the modern viewer's sense of optical displacement is reinforced by some seemingly minor, arbitrary gesture which further detaches the scene from representational fact. In *The Bar at the Folies-Bergère* this occurs in the way Manet paints two gaslights reflected in the mirror; they are disks of pure white, white disks which lie flat on the picture plane; these lanterns cast no shadow, they show no penumbral refractions as mirrored lights usually do, nor indeed are they even painted in the round. Again, Manet's contemporaries found in these strange lights a sign of the painter's weakness. In *L'Illustration*, Jules Compte remarked of them that 'Monsieur Manet has probably chosen a moment when the lamps were not working properly, for never have we seen light less dazzling . . .'[2]

Today we can see these white disks serve the same purpose as the displaced reflection of the barmaid's black dress. They set up the painting so that we focus on the only significant experience of depth and recession in it. In the upper right corner of the painting, reflected in the mirror, we see the man the barmaid is looking at, staring intently into her eyes.

However, just as the barmaid's back cannot possibly be reflected to her immediate right, this intent gentleman in his top hat, asking her a question with his eyes, who inspires in her a look of such sadness, cannot optically exist, for he would entirely block out our direct, unobstructed view of Suzon, who is in turn looking straight in front of her. The painting is set up so that the viewer, you or me, is standing in front of her. But of course you or I don't resemble the particular person reflected in the mirror. Due to the full-frontal positioning of the subject in relation to the viewer, there is no way to look at her without this reflexive disturbance occurring. The drama Manet creates in this painting is: I look in a mirror and see someone who is not myself.

This aspect of the painting did speak to Manet's contemporaries. Some sought to pass off the disturbance with a joke (the *Journal Amusant* of 27 May 1882 made a woodcut of the painting with the gentleman reflected in the mirror drawn in, standing before the barmaid and blocking our view), but most critics reacted with anger to the disturbing questions about the viewer created by Manet's painting: 'Is this picture true? No. Is it beautiful? No. Is it attractive? No. But what is it, then?'[3] Their distress could have mostly had to do with the story being told by the painting; a man propositions a young barmaid, who responds to him with a look of infinite sadness.

Of course such a story is as apt a Victorian homily as one could imagine. The lonely young woman in a vice-tainted public realm was a homily Edgar Degas painted more directly, for instance, in *L'Absinthe* of 1876. In Manet's painting the optic disturbance relieves the woman of serving such a neatly moralizing purpose. A question is raised about the story of the painting by making the viewing of the painting, by men and women in other costumes, times, and places, inseparable from the story being told. In the same painterly way, the objects placed on the bar are given a heightened life. The bottles on the bar are painted fully in the round; they contrast to the abstract disks in that mirror which shows us another self than the one we might prefer to call our own. Although the mirror runs full length across the painting, Manet allows only two of this crowded collection of objects to show in reflection, even though optically *all* should show. These optical ghosts of bottles, flowers and fruit seem the most solid objects in the painting.

This is how displacement works in *The Bar at the Folies-Bergère*. Displacement creates value: both reflexive value, that is a value given to the viewer as part of the thing seen, and again to the physical world itself, whose character and form we are forced to assess by looking at its transmutation in a distorting mirror. By contrast, there is but an illusory solidity to those objects which have not been subjected to this displacement. Were Manet a philosopher – which he emphatically would protest he was not – he might point to this as the real point of his painting: the solidity of undisplaced things, as of selves which have not experienced displacement, may indeed be the greatest of illusions. This painting certainly makes a modernist promise: disturbance will infuse value into experience. But how could this promise of displacement be kept off the canvas, in the street?

A Change in Exile

Were we able to walk the streets of Paris in Manet's youth – the streets contained between the Rue de Rivoli and the Boulevard Saint-Germain north to south, and what are now the bridges of Saint Michel and Carrousel east to west – we might see the method of Manet's painting setting one scene of life.

In this section of Paris were contained a crowd of foreigners mixed among the students of the Beaux-Arts and the medical and law faculties of the University of Paris. The largest and oldest contingent were central Europeans, Poles and Bohemians who had been steadily displaced from their homelands in the 1830s. Throughout the 1840s Italian political émigrés poured into this part of the city, joined in 1846 by a contingent of Greeks. Most were in Paris because of their politics at home; most were intellectuals, though the Greeks included a large number of sailors who had been caught up in the war of independence a generation before.

We might think of this as a pre-modern world of foreigners. The Parisians idealized the resistance of local burghers elsewhere to aristocratic and royal exploitation. Though a people not notably accessible to outsiders, the French thus received the Poles and later the Greeks warmly; the upheavals in both these countries were perceived as middle-class revolts rather than upheavals of the poor. During the 1830s the universities of France were opened to foreigners, and the right of political asylum was first codified in its modern form (in which an individual can apply for this status through an established state bureaucracy, rather than plead for it as favour from a ruler). Under these conditions the émigrés of the 1830s and 1840s sought to mobilize the Parisians on behalf of their various causes, hoping to gain both money and the pressure of public opinion which would in turn move the French government to act. Today, we know the fashionable side of these efforts, such as the music Chopin wrote as *pièces d'occasion* for charity concerts, but there was a more popular enlistment of the public, as in the proselytizing of the Greek sailors among the stevedores and carters of the *quais* of the Seine for aid; they were so successful that Greek work costumes were worn on the docks as a sign of sympathy. Moreover, the Paris police on the whole approved, thinking foreign interests would deflect French workers from local discontents, a deflection of the Parisian proletariat which had worked effectively throughout the Napoleonic Wars.

It was, as I say, a curious situation, this xenophobic nation who found persecuted foreigners attractive, but it was also a historically pregnant scene. For it is in Paris that there first became apparent those changes which would produce the more modern image of the foreigner as a figure necessarily in pain. These changes, paradoxically, are due to the development of modern nationalism; nationalism made those who leave their nations seem like surgical patients who have suffered an amputation.

It is of course true that from the Greeks onwards belonging to a nation has been thought necessary to forming a whole human being; the foreigners in the Greek city-states – the metics – were considered by citizens to be slightly juvenile, since they could not excercise the adult privilege of voting. But the meanings of a 'nation' have changed greatly in the course of Western history; at times nationality has been inseparable from a particular religious practice, at times defined by aristocratic dynasties, at times including the net of trading partners of a mother city.

The nationalism which began to find its voice in the Revolution of 1848 marks a distinct version of collective identity in our civilization: nationality becomes an anthropological phenomenon to which political activity is, at best, a servant: the nation becomes an *ethos*, the rule of *nomos* in Greek terms; that is, the sheer rule of custom; and it is almost crime to interfere with the sacredness of custom through political decision-making or diplomatic negotiation. It was due to this great change in the meaning of nationality that the exiles who lived in Paris in 1848 would find themselves having to rethink what it meant to be long displaced from 'home'. Their everyday lives abroad gradually lost contact with the rituals and customs of the homeland, the *nomos* becoming a memory rather than an activity. They would have to find a meaning for their lives in the very fact of their displacement, in being foreigners: they would need to look at their memories of the nation in something like Manet's mirror.

The Revolution of 1848 lasted four months, from February to June of that year. It began in Paris, but by March its repercussions were felt throughout Central Europe, where movements sprang up proclaiming the superiority of national republics over the geographic parcellings of territory made by dynasties and diplomats at the Congress of Vienna in 1815. Events had something of the same combustive character as did the disengagement from

Russian hegemony which spread across these same nations in the last four months of 1989.

The doctrinaires of 'the nation' who began to make a public impression in 1848 used a different kind of language from those who had earlier argued for constitutional regimes, democracy or other political ideals in their homelands, echoing the ideals of the American and French Revolutions. The language of the Slavophiles or the Sons of Attica was, as I say, a triumph of anthropology over politics. In 1848, the idea of a nation as a political codex was rejected by the revolutionary nationalists because they believed that a nation was enacted instead by custom, by the manners and mores of a *volk*: the food people eat, how they move when they dance, the dialects they speak, the precise forms of their prayers, these are the constituent elements of national life. Law is incapable of legislating these pleasures in certain foods, constitutions cannot ordain fervent belief in certain saints: that is, power cannot make culture.

The doctrine of nationalism which crystallized in 1848 gives a geographic imperative to the concept of culture itself: habit, faith, pleasure, ritual – all depend upon enactment in a particular territory. More, the place which nourishes rituals is a place composed of people like oneself, people with whom one can share without explaining. Territory thus becomes synonymous with identity.

It is important to understand that the annals

of mid-nineteenth-century Europe were filled with revolutionary nationalists preaching to a sometimes receptive, sometimes indifferent public, but always a public which was hearing something new: it heard ordinary rituals and beliefs praised, and everyday life celebrated, as collective virtue. An older code of national honour, for instance, would have found this celebration of everyday life degrading. In that older code, you placed a foot soldier in a blue-and-red flannel uniform fitted with gold braid, epaulettes and stamped ceremonial buttons. No matter that it was a useless costume or worse than useless during military engagement, no matter that he might be starving in barracks; this ceremonial robe gave him a place in something greater and grander than himself, it glorified his condition as a Frenchman. Similarly, in peacetime monarchs like Louis XIV sought to legitimate their policies through elaborate ceremonies; these 'progresses', 'turnings' and 'audiences' threw into dramatic relief the glory of the state, its magnificent constructions elevated far above, and so 'unnatural' in relation to, the sphere of everyday life. National honour was to be found in artifice.

By contrast, the ideology of the nation preached by Kossuth, Manzoni, Garibaldi, Mickiewitz or Louis Blanc – that the people should glory in their ordinary selves as they were marketing, feasting, praying, harvesting – meant that honour was to be found in authenticity rather than in artifice.

The spirit of this new nationalism makes its appearance visually almost as soon as the revolutionary texts are printed in February and March of 1848. In the posters calling for national unity composed in the spring of 1848 by Chodluz and others, the People are shown responding to the call for uprising dressed in work clothes, or in peasant costume. This imagery is more complicated than simply identifying the People with the poor, for in the revolutionary posters of 1790 and 1791 the poor were often depicted in military uniforms, or wearing the colours of their political clubs. Two generations later, in responding to a great historical event, the People do not dress for the occasion. Nor in the posters of 1848 are the masses given especially dramatic expressions of rage or patriotic zeal: everything is done to signify that the people are not self-conscious, just being themselves. Gone, indeed, are even the allegorical, classical figures who emblazoned the posters of the revolutions of 1830, such as Delacroix's *Liberty Leading the People*. For the revolutionary nationalists of 1848, the unawareness of the *volk* of itself, its lack of a mirror, was a source of virtue – as against the vices of self-consciousness and self-estrangement of the cosmopolitan bourgeois whose mental outlook is upon a diorama of mirrors which reflect back endless hesitations and second thoughts.

This anthropological image of a *volk* is an epochal event in modern social imagery and rhetoric.

Nineteenth-century nationalism established what we might call the modern ground-rule for having an identity. You have the strongest identity when you aren't aware you 'have' it; you just *are* it. That is, you are most yourself when you are least aware of yourself.

It is important to understand this formula is indeed a rule for excercising power, even though it speaks in the name of a cultural unity, a folk soul, beyond the reach of any political regime. The great imperialists of the nineteenth century, men like Livingstone, Stanley and Rhodes, subscribed to this anthropological view; they too held the widespread view of the sacred character of everyday culture, they believed in the primacy of *nomos*; only they derived from it the principle that 'natives' should not be contaminated by too much contact with the foreign masters, or the integrity of native culture will be diminished. Rhodes was in earnest. It is simply that the ground-rule of modern *nomos*, that you are most yourself when you are least aware of yourself, can be made to serve both revolutionary upheaval, as in 1848, or orchestrate the forms by which one nation dominates others yet seeks to prevent cultural 'contamination'. In the same way a modern state can also capitalize upon anthropological virtue. Its institutions can be legitimated as reflections of popular impulse rather than as *constructions* which might be problematic and in need of constant discussion.

Institutions like the civil police or the neighbourhood revolutionary committee can be declared permanent organs of spontaneity, the consequences of what 'everybody' wants welling up from the folk-life.

Rousseau's celebration of 'the noble savage' a century before 1848 was a bitter play on words. Rousseau seems to have been much struck by the stuffed figure of an American Indian in full ceremonial dress who was put on display in Paris by a taxidermist in 1741; this 'savage' Rousseau imagined to be a man whose reflectiveness was more acute and profound than the bewigged, gossipy, thoughtless Parisians who came to the taxidermist's shop. The Noble Savage – the eighteenth century's idealization of the authentic person – thinks. Again, the divide between the eighteenth-century revolutionaries and the nineteenth-century nationalists was marked by a difference in geographic consciousness. The political doctrines of 1789 transcended place; one did not have to live in Paris, or to be French, to believe in the liberty, equality and fraternity proclaimed in the French Revolution. Or again, Kant in his *Reflections of a Universal Citizen of the World* of 1784 argued that a human being develops the more a person feels at home and derives stimulation among a diversity of other people. This 'universal citizen' seeks the stimulation of foreign scenes, and learns what is common, universal, in them all.

Of course no change in ideology occurs as a simple switch from one form of belief to another. In Manzoni's writings on the Italian peasantry, his rural countrymen sometimes appear as the real Italians because, removed from the cities which were the seats of Austro-Hungarian power, they have guarded the practices of an earlier, free Italy. In this they are like Rousseau's noble savage – self-conscious guardians of what is in fact a superior culture. And then, sometimes Manzoni writes as Tolstoy will later write, the peasantry is morally superior because peasants have no awareness of themselves in time and history, are free of the gnawing poison of too much thought, of thinking beyond the confines of life as it is given. The peasant does not look in the mirror of history; he simply is. The People are silent.

In the rhetoric of nationalism which took form in the nineteenth century, the spontaneity and lack of cosmopolitan self-consciousness of the people was linked in turn to a conception of national time. The nation also, simply, is. The rhetoric of nationalism took a people's rituals, beliefs and mores to represent forms of being rather than doing, to make Heidegger's distinction; the rituals, beliefs and mores which create the national ideal are celebrated as time-tested and permanently cohering – they belong to the very land, to the unity of human beings with 'their' soil. This notion of national being also entails a certain kind of silence. In Louis Kossuth's appeals for a Magyar revolt, the centuries-long interaction of Magyars with the Turks, Slavs and Germans whom history had brought among them is excluded from the account of what it is to be Magyar; these historic encounters in fact coloured the practice of religion, created a complex cuisine, and altered the structure of the Hungarian language itself. In place of this history, Kossuth preached a version of Magyar culture as if from generation to generation it had been both unchanging and self-sustaining. The corollary of national time, a time of being, was the concept of national purity.

As Isaiah Berlin has shown in his study *Vico and Herder*, those two eighteenth-century forerunners of nineteenth-century nationalism, the framing of the nation in anthropological terms began for the most liberal of all reasons; it was an affirmation of the dignity of human differences. For Herder, in Berlin's words, '. . . it is [people's] differences that matter most for it is the differences that make them what they are, make them themselves.'[4] It is easy to forget how bold and how recent is the very assertion that human beings are creatures of particular cultures. Machiavelli whispered advice into his prince's ear drawing upon examples of ancient emperors and kings; these rulers dead for thousands of years could yet serve the prince as models because human nature does not change, or so Machiavelli and his contemporaries thought.

The assertion that human beings are culture-specific was in the eighteenth century again more than a plea for taking anthropological variation seriously. It was an attack upon what we call today 'Eurocentrism'. Voltaire believed that 'It is terrible arrogance to affirm that, to be happy, everyone should become European.'[5] In different places, different people find different ways to attempt happiness, that most difficult of feats. Yet the break between the affirmation of difference in the eighteenth century and its affirmation in the nineteenth lay just here: to Voltaire, the knowledge that others do not die of foods we are afraid to eat, that others in fact find happiness in tasting them, ought to give us pause about our own convictions, indeed ought to arouse our desire to taste the forbidden. The perception of differing values ought to make the perceiver more cosmpolitan. Whereas Herder understood something ahead of his time: the perception of difference might make people more ethnocentric, since there is no common humanity to which they can jointly appeal.

Place and displace; the virtue of being yourself in place, and the vice of looking at yourself somewhere else. Just here the problems of being a foreigner began. In the early spring of 1848, it seemed to Parisians like 'Daniel Stern' (the nom de plume of Marie d'Agoult, Franz Liszt's one-time companion whose chronicles of 1848 are a vivid record of the upheaval) that the 'foreign colony will empty in a few days, as our friends return to the places which call them'.[6] Given the nationalisms being trumped in the press, her expectation seems logical. The political question this nationalism posed to all those who had become foreigners – émigrés, ex-patriots or exiles – is, why aren't you home among your own kind? How indeed could you be Russian, somewhere else? Yet by late April of 1848 Daniel Stern had noted that, oddly, few of the émigrés had left for home. 'They are still to be found arguing in the Palais Royal, receiving emissaries from abroad, hectoring; they are full of hope, but no one has packed his bags.'[7]

Perhaps the greatest of nineteenth-century exiles was a man who would make but a brief appearance on this scene yet, from observing it, would capture in indelible prose the cursed relation between nationalism and the condition of being a foreigner. Alexander Herzen was the illegitimate son of an ageing Russian nobleman and a young German woman (hence his name, which is roughly equivalent to *herzlich*, 'of my heart'). Inspired by the uprising of 1825, he was as a young man active in radical Russian politics as these politics were then understood; that is, he was a proponent of constitutional monarchy and liberal reforms. For this he suffered internal exile and eventually expulsion from the Russian Empire. Like others of his generation, he thought of himself at first as in temporary exile, expecting to return to his native land when political circumstances made it possible. But when at last this possibility arose, he held back. It was not out of social assimilation or love for European culture or personal ties – like those of his friend Turgenev to Pauline Viardot – which kept him from returning. He remained passionately interested in the affairs of his country but felt no longer able to live in it. He perambulated the capitals of Western Europe, passing his later years in London, where he published a famous newsletter about Russian realities called *The Bell*.

There is a certain kind of social thinking, falsely humane, which posits an inverse relation between consciousness and circumstance. In this kind of thinking, the sufferings of the poor make them intellectual victims of their necessities; poor thought is the sheer calculation of survival. The niceties of consciousness, the complexities of interpretation, are seen as luxuries of the affluent. In this way of thinking, the bastard son of an aristocrat can be no guide to the dilemmas faced by the wave upon wave of emigrants who would quit Europe in the nineteenth century, much less a guide for the conundrums faced by Mexican day workers, Korean grocers, Soviet Jews or other foreigners today. Herzen the friend of John Stuart Mill, diffident with the diffidence bred of attending many formal occasions;

Herzen so curious about the places in which yet he knew he did not belong . . . Herzen enters this story in April of 1848. It was at this moment of delay that Herzen joined the exile colony in Paris; he did so to move away from Rome, which was in its own first moments of nationalist awakening.

It must not be thought that Herzen or the other Parisian émigrés who did not immediately respond to the call of their own nation were cowards; the lives of many émigrés read as a long series of prior imprisonments and tortures, particularly at the hands of the Austrian police. In part the answer to their immobility was to be found in a familiar cruelty, that of events passing them by. Their web of mutual contacts abroad was outdated, just as their political plans for constitutions and government agencies had no place in the new rhetoric of the People. But more than this, as Daniel Stern noted, something had happened to the foreigners themselves in exile. 'It is as though they have looked in the mirror and seen another face than the one they thought they would see,' she wrote.[8] It puzzled the émigrés, as well as her: something in them resisted returning, something held them back.

Her image strikingly recalls Manet's mirror, in which what is reflected back to us is so unlike what we expect to see. It was exactly this connection which Herzen would in the course of his life take up, seeking to understand how nationalism had forced people to look in something like Manet's mirror to find a liveable, humane image of themselves. Ritual, belief, habit, and the signs of language would appear far different in this displacing mirror than at home. The foreigner might indeed have a more intelligent, more humane relation to his or her culture than the person who has never moved, who knows nothing but that which is, who has not been obliged to ponder the differences of one culture from another. But that is not the pressing business of becoming a foreigner. It is rather that one has to deal creatively with one's own displaced condition, deal with the materials of identity the way an artist has to deal with the dumb facts which are things to be painted. One has to make oneself.

This was, at least, the possibility that Herzen sensed, reading newspaper accounts of a wave of violence in Slovakia directed against the gypsies who had poured into the country, the gypsies believing in 1848 as in 1990 that a nation which rises against its masters might promise them freedom as well; Herzen sipping wine in the Café Lamblin which even a century and a half later serves that beverage in the adulterated form which disgusted him; Herzen's companions plotting, telegraphing, arguing, and remaining; Herzen leading a foreign contingent in a march on the National Assembly, in support of the 'rights of man'. They would have to find a new way to be Russian.

The Second Scar

The fact on which the entire story in the legend of Oedipus the King turns seems of little artistic interest in itself, rather just a cog in the machinery of the plot. There was a physical mark on the king's ankles resulting from a wound he received as a child. The name 'Oedipus' itself means in Greek 'one with pierced ankles'. The king has wandered, lost touch with his origins; when the characters in the legend come to the point where they must know the king's true identity, they are able to recover this truth by looking at his body. The process of identification begins when a messenger declares: 'Your ankles should be witnesses.'[9]

Were the evidence King Oedipus seeking not about incest, we might pay more attention to his scar. Despite the great migrations in his life, his body contains permanent evidence about who he 'really' is. The king's travels have left no comparable signatures upon his body. His migratory experience counts for little, that is, in relation to his origin. This scar of Oedipus seems a source in Western culture for the indelible marks which the nineteenth century would read on the collective body of the nation. Origin becomes destiny. Indeed, it might seem, looking back to the beginnings of our civilization, that exile, dispossession, migration, have been of far lesser account than the marks of origins and of belonging. One would think of Socrates' refusal of exile as evidence of the belief that even death as a citizen was more honorable than exile. Or Thucydides' remark that foreigners have no speech, by which is meant not that they literally don't know how to talk well but that their speech counts for little in the polis; it is the chattering of those who can't vote.

And yet the marks on Oedipus' ankles will not be the only marks on his body. He will answer the wounds others made on him at the beginning by gouging his own eyes out. If we cast the sexual weight of this legend aside and examine it simply as a story, the second wound balances the first; the first is a wound marking his origins, the second marking his subsequent history. Twice-wounded, he has become a man whose life can literally be read on his body, and in this condition he sets out again into the world as a wanderer. Oedipus thinks in leaving Thebes that perhaps he could return to his origins, to the mountain, '... *my* mountain, which my mother and my father while they were living would have made my tomb',[10] yet this return is not to be. As *Oedipus at Colonus* opens, he has come instead to the deme (village) of Colonus, a mile north-west of Athens, where the Delphic oracle has told him he will die instead; the prophecy will in turn be fulfilled differently than he had imagined at the opening of the play. The two wounds on Oedipus' body are thus a scar of origins which cannot be concealed and the wanderer's scars which do not seem to heal.

This second, unhealing scar signifies in Western civilization as much as does the scar of origin, which marks the value placed on membership in a particular place. The Greeks themselves would have understood Oedipus' unending journey as resonant with the Homeric legends, particularly the legend of Odysseus. In Greek practice, later to be codified in Roman law, there were certain circumstances in which foreign exile was in fact honourable, more honourable than Socrates' way; *exsilium* entitled the person convicted of a capital charge to choose exile instead of death, a choice which spared friends and family the shame and grief of witnessing one's execution. But Sophocles in *Oedipus at Colonus* introduces a moral dimension to the very act of migration, in depicting Oedipus as a figure who has been ennobled by his uprooting. The play makes of Oedipus the *metic*, the foreigner, a figure of tragic grandeur rather than an outsider lesser in stature than a citizen.

Becoming a foreigner means displacement from one's roots. Such uprooting has a positive moral value, indeed is central to the Judeo-Christian tradition. The people of the Old Testament thought of themselves as uprooted wanderers.[11] The Yahweh of the Old Testament was himself a wandering god, his Ark of the Covenant portable and, in the theologian

Harvey Cox's words, 'When the Ark was finally captured by the Philistines, the Hebrews began to realize that Yahweh was not localized even in it . . . He traveled with his people and elsewhere.'[12] Yahweh was a god of time rather than of place, a god who promised to his followers a divine meaning for their unhappy travels.

Wandering and exposure were as strongly felt to be the consequences of faith among early Christians as among Old Testament Jews. The author of the *Epistle to Diognatus* at the height of the Roman Empire's glory declared that

> Christians are not distinguished from the rest of humanity either in locality or in speech or in customs. For they do not dwell oft in cities of their own . . . nor do they practice an extraordinary style of life . . . they dwell in their own countries, but only as sojourners . . . Every foreign country is a fatherland to them, and every fatherland is a foreign country.[13]

This image of the wanderer came to be one of the ways in which St Augustine defined the two cities in *The City of God*:

> Now it is recorded of Cain that he built a city, while Abel, as though he were merely a pilgrim on earth, built none. For the true City of the saints is in heaven, though here on earth it

produces citizens in which it wanders as though on a pilgrimage through time looking for the Kingdom of eternity.[14]

This 'pilgrimage through time' rather than settling in place draws its authority from Jesus' refusal to allow His disciples to build monuments to Him, and His promise to destroy the Temple of Jerusalem. Judeo-Christian culture is thus, at its very sources, about experiences of displacement. Ours is a religious culture of the second scar.

The reason for this value put upon uprooting derives from a deeply-felt distrust of the anthropology of everyday life; *nomos* is not truth. Ordinary things, in themselves, are illusory – as illusory to the Orphics and to Plato as they were to St Augustine. Such a devaluation of everyday behaviour appears at the haunting moment in *Oedipus Coloneus* in the speech Oedipus makes to the young Theseus:

> Dear son of Aegeus, to the gods alone it happens never to die or to grow old; all else is confounded by almighty Time. The strength of the land wastes away, and the strength of the body; faith dies and faithlessness comes to be, and the same wind blows not with constancy either in the friendships of men or between city and city. To some now, and to others later, the sweet becomes bitter and then again pleasant. And if in Thebes it is now fair weather for you, Time in his

course will break to pieces the present pledges of harmony for a small word's sake.[15]

This second scar which is the mark of the foreigner is a moral stigmata, then, precisely because it does not heal. In both Classical and Judeo-Christian thought, those who have cut free from circumstance, who lead uprooted lives, can become consequent human beings. Wandering the world, they transformed themselves. They set themselves free from blind participation, and thus could enquire searchingly, could make choices for themselves, or, like the blind Greek king and the Christian martyr, feel at last in the presence of a Higher Power. The two scars on the body of King Oedipus represent a fundamental conflict in our civilization between the truth-claims of place and beginnings versus the truths to be discovered in becoming a foreigner.

This is the context in which should be set the passions of modern nationalism, with its emphasis on sharing among similar people, the dignity of everyday life, the value of identity. These passions argue for community at the expense of self-transformation. From the Homeric legends through the tragic playwrights, from the prophets of the Old Testament through the early Christian prelates, there has been a contrary passion for self-transforming experiences at the expense of community, a passion for displacement.

Herzen's Mirror

On 27 June 1848, the Revolution came to an end in Paris. Troops swept through the city indiscriminately shooting into crowds, deploying cannon in random barrages into working-class neighbourhoods; the forces of order had arrived. Herzen, like the other foreigners who had remained in Paris of their own free will, were now forced to leave; he went to Geneva, then back to Italy, then back to France, arriving finally in London in August of 1852, an ailing middle-aged man whose wife was erotically engaged elsewhere, who had set himself publicly against the Slavophiles dominating radical discourse in his homeland, who spoke English haltingly in the manner of novels he had read by Sir Walter Scott. '[L]ittle by little I began to perceive that I had absolutely nowhere to go and no reason to go anywhere.'[16] It is not inflating his suffering to say that at this moment Herzen became something like a tragic figure, a man who felt the second scar of homelessness which will not heal.

What is instructive about Herzen's writings is the sense he comes to make about how to conduct daily life in such a condition, how to make sense of being a foreigner. ' . . . By degrees, a revolution took place within me.' In part he began to make a virtue of his very isolation in exile: 'I was conscious of power in myself . . . I grew more independent of everyone.'[17] And so he began to reconstruct how he saw the world around him: '[N]ow the masquerade was over, the dominoes had been removed, the garlands had fallen from the heads, the masks from the faces . . .' To explain the consequences of this new vision of others in this personal crisis of exile Herzen resorted to the same imagery of displaced vision that Daniel Stern had evoked. 'I saw features different from those that I had surmised.'[18]

Rather than making of his exile a reason for spiritual transcendence of the world itself, as a Christian might, Herzen stayed on the ground; he tried to understand how a foreigner should cope with his or her own nationality. The nation, for a person who had become a foreigner, posed two dangers, one a danger of forgetting, the other of remembering; the one a condition in which the foreigner was demeaned by the desire to assimilate, the other in which he or she was destroyed by nostalgia.

In his own experience Herzen came in the 1850s to see these dangers exemplified by two men who came from his past in the 1830s and the early 1840s. Ivan Golovin was, like Herzen, a political refugee of those years, but he had at first seemed to Herzen simply a despicable individual, a small-time crook barred after a few years from the Paris stock exchange, an exploiter of his fellow exiles, flitting from scene to scene. Herzen now came to see his personal vices magnified by the conduct of his exile: 'What had he left Russia for? What was he doing in Europe? . . . Uprooted from his native soil, he could not find a center of gravity.'[19] The importance of Golovin's character was magnified in Herzen's reflections in London. Golovin's character, Herzen wrote, 'bears the stamp of a whole class of people', those whose very desire to assimilate had led to a loss of self:

> . . . who live nomadic lives, with cards or without cards at spaces and in great cities, invariably dining well, known by everybody, and about whom everything is known, except two things: what they live on and what they live for. Golovin was a Russian office, a French *braider* and *hobbler*, an English swindler, a German Junker, as well as our native Nozdrev Khlestakov [character from Gogol] . . .[20]

Abroad, such people see that their new compatriots cannot understand what it was like in the place one came from, or it does not interest them – understandably so, it is all so far away, so long ago, in a word so foreign. And so men like Golovin, afraid to risk alienating or boring the others, act as though it never was.

Herzen was much too civilized to look at those foreigners seeking to assimilate as necessarily morally tainted. He looked at them rather as people who were engaged in a kind of voluntary amnesia, and he feared that, from this will to forget, could come other acts of denial. In the painting the foreigner is making of his or her life, large patches are over-painted in white.

One might perhaps reformulate the insight Herzen had in looking at Golovin as follows: the desire for assimilation can be experienced as a force which creates a sense of shame about oneself, and so weakens one's ego strength. Of course the capacity to assimilate requires income, educational and occupational advantages that an aspiring 'new American', say, is likely to lack. But a person consumed by the desire to assimilate may also behave like a self-censor, screening out the full range of experiences and observations which he or she has lived; self-screening supposes there is something shameful, unacceptable in one's past, to be kept from others. For the foreigner this cycle of censorship and shame can begin with nothing more than feeling that the gesture of touching others when one talks to them, or the smell of foreign foods on one's breath, are behaviours which must be corrected. Shame about the fact that one's breath smells different when one eats foods from the old country is reinforced by the very fear of breathing into the faces of people who do not eat these foods. Feeling ashamed of oneself is indeed likely to lead to the loss of judgement, if not moral probity, which Herzen observed in Golovin. It is why, for us, the famous 'melting pot' of American myth may function more like a meltdown of the ego's ethical powers.[21]

Golovin is a significant figure in Herzen's own attempt to work out what it means to be Russian, somewhere else – the attempt to understand how to make a humane displacement of one's nationality. In a famous letter Golovin wrote to the editor of the *Moscow News* from Paris on 1 February 1866, he declared, 'I was a man before I was a Russian.'[22] Herzen prints this letter at the very end of his portrait of Golovin – and indeed of the first edition of *My Past and Thoughts*. The irony is meant to resonate. Such a declaration in the Age of Enlightenment could come from Kant; now it comes from a stock-speculator and extortion artist, anxious only to fit in wherever he is. The revelations of exile surely cannot end this way. For the foreigner, the knowledge that he comes from elsewhere, rather than being a source of shame, should be a cautionary knowledge.

For Herzen, economic individualism was the great danger of the era of capitalist expansion he saw coming into being. Nationalism and capitalism could march hand in hand, as Herzen, a confirmed socialist, argued again and again in *The Bell*. By contrast, Herzen's hopes for a socialist movement were pinned on immigrants. Their very displacement gave them the experience, or at least the possibility, of looking beyond themselves, dealing with others similarly displaced in a cooperative fashion.

As a reader of Herzen, it is here that I find him at his most compelling. Herzen would have thought it perfectly comprehensible that ethnic groups in modern America were at the centre of liberalism of the American kind, feeble version of democratic socialism in Europe that it is. He would have explained this relation between immigration and liberality, I think, by saying that the scars of displacement had liberally disposed those aware of themselves as foreigners, unlike the Golovins who seek only to forget. Herzen's belief that socialism is most practicable by foreigners is an idealization of displacement, to be sure, but an ideal founded on a profound and profoundly sceptical doubt that the evils of possessive individualism could ever be cured by communal relations of the nationalist, homogeneous, self-referential sort. Only the knowledge of difference and the experience of displacement can erect a barrier of experience to the appetites of possessive individualism.

In reading Herzen as a writer about our own times in germ, one needs to think about distinction between liberalism and pluralism. The modern ground-rule of identity threatens constantly to restrict personal freedom to cultural practice: your needs are legitimate insofar as they can be identified with what the Mexican community, or elderly Russians, or young black women, *do*. The liberal ideal can be degraded into mere pluralism through a particular application of this rule: pluralism becomes simply a matter of defining the borders between communities sharing abutting territories; within each, people live as though they have never left home, as though nothing has happened. Paradoxically, it is the vivid consciousness of oneself as a foreigner which is necessary to defeat this pluralist self-enclosure in ethnicity. Herzen recalls someone in England saying to him, '"In your words," a very worthy man said to me, "one hears an outside spectator speaking." But I did not come to Europe as an outsider, you know. An outsider is what I have become.'[23] And for this same reason, in their recent book *Immigrant America* Alejandro Portes and Ruben Rumbaut flatly declare, 'Assimilation as the rapid transformation of immigrants into Americans "as everyone else" has never happened.'[24] Their assertion is more than a sociological observation; it is the affirmation of a necessary, enlightened consciousness.

Nostalgia, the opposite danger of amnesia, seems a simpler condition. Indeed it seemed so to Herzen in Geneva in 1850 just after he had quit Paris with the other Central European refugees. For the first time it dawned on many of them that they were in permanent exile, which triggered in them the dangers of nostalgia:

> All *émigrés*, cut off from the living environment to which they have belonged, shut their eyes to avoid seeing bitter truths, and grow more and more acclimatized to a closed, fantastic circle consisting of inert memories and hopes that can never be realized . . .

and again,

> Leaving their native land with concealed anger, with the continual thought of going back to it once more on the morrow, men do not move forwards but are continually thrown back upon the past . . .

From which he concluded that the exile could be enslaved as well by his or her own powers of memory, those 'questions, thoughts and memories which make up an oppressive, binding tradition'.[25]

Fifteen years later, in London, Herzen takes up again in his memoirs the subject of émigré nostalgia, and now it too is transformed by his own transformation in exile. Herzen writes of his encounters with Father Vladimir Pecherin in a short portrait worthy of Chekhov. Pecherin is someone Herzen, like all people of his generation, knew about. In the middle of the 1830s the young Pecherin had taken up the Chair of Greek at Moscow University, and felt himself in the next few years suffocating in his homeland; in Herzen's words, '[R]ound about was silence and solitude: everything was dumb submission with no hope, no human dignity, and at the same time extraordinarily, dull, stupid and petty.'[26] Pecherin, the young Classics professor, decided to emigrate, which surprised none of his contemporaries who were also suffocating in Mother Russia; Pecherin boarded a boat for England, landed . . . and suddenly entered a Jesuit monastery. In this he did surprise other young people around him, who could not understand how he could revolt against one system of authority only to submit to another.

When Herzen landed in England he sought out Pecherin, to make his acquaintance and to ask if some of Pecherin's youthful poems might be reprinted in Herzen's publication *The Bell*. They meet in the Jesuit monastery of Saint Mary's, Clapham; the two Russians begin by speaking French to one another, then, though Pecherin fears he can hardly remember his mother tongue, in Russian. Pecherin is avid for news, he disowns the value of his Russian poems yet is eager for the younger man's opinion. After their meeting, they begin to correspond, the Jesuit convert writing in French about materialism, science and faith, writing with intensity to this stranger, assuming no boundaries stand between their full exposure to one another – as no Frenchman, whether devout or not, would presume to do.

Herzen tells us all this as preparation for recounting an event he read in the newspapers two years later, in 1855. A Jesuit monk, described in the press as a 'Reverend Father Wladimir Petcherine, a native of Russian', was on trial for burning a Protestant Bible in a marketplace in an Irish town. Here is Herzen's digest of what happened at the trial: 'The proud British judge, taking into consideration the senselessness of the action and the fact that the accused was a Russian, and England and Russia were at war [the Crimean War], confined himself to a paternal exhortation to decent behavior in the streets in future . . .'[27]

Even more fascinating than the story Herzen recounts is the fact that he has got it all wrong by 1865, when he came to write this part of his memoirs. In point of fact, Pecherin showed that he had caused some pornographic literature to be burnt, not a Bible, and he was acquitted. The sensation at the time was about a Jesuit taking 'direct action' when discovering smut; the future Prime Minister Gladstone, much interested in the conditions of prostitution in modern England, was for one intrigued by this 'direct action' against pornography. There is a reason for Herzen in recalling it to alter (I do not suppose with conscious intent to deceive) the story of Pecherin's trial. For to Herzen this is a story of how those displaced from their homelands can remain prisoners of the past. It makes perfect sense to Herzen: a Russian messenger arrives who will print evidence of Pecherin's past life, the life of a young man passed in Moscow when Tsar Nicholas, abetted by the clergy, had organized police searches in the universities for heretical writings. For Herzen, the point of the story is that Pecherin suffered something like an atavistic seizure. The youthful victim of orthodoxy has become a policeman of heresy.

Pecherin is an exemplary figure of a disaster which Herzen has come to observe with ever greater fear during his years of exile: it is what Freud was later to call the 'return of the repressed.'[28] The return of the repressed is of far greater danger to the foreigner than explicit longing for the past. This return of the repressed befalls those who do not work to transform that part of themselves which lives in memory. The foreigner must confront memories of home; memory must be displaced, refracted, so that he or she is not suddenly seized by the past, acting out the injuries received long ago, now playing instead another role in that old drama. But how is a transformation to occur so that the drama itself is rewritten?

The advice which gradually takes form in the pages of Herzen's memoir about how to behave in the countries where the foreigner lives is something like: 'Participate, but do not identify.' This admonition suggests how a foreigner may defeat the segregating game of pluralism. The impulse to participate is an assertion that one has rights as a political animal, a *zóon politikón*, wherever one lives. In place of the ancient device, 'nothing that is human is foreign to me', the device of modern identity could be, 'nothing that is foreign to me is real'. The Japanese President Nakasone once asserted: 'Only those who understand one another can make decisions together.'[29] A foreigner's assertion of the right to participate, beyond what pertains to his or her national identity, is one way to force the dominant society to acknowledge that there is, on the contrary, a public sphere beyond the borders of anthropology. It is also the only way to survive being personally imprisoned in a Balkanized, unequal city of differences. Herzen found a way to create a picture of 'home' so as to make bearable his very yearning for it. In London, he says, suddenly he has become Italian:

> And now I sit in London where chance has flung me – and I stay here because I do not know what to make of myself. An alien race swarms confusedly about me, wrapped in the heavy breath of ocean, a world dissolving into chaos . . . and that other land – washed by the dark-blue sea under the canopy of a dark-blue sky . . . it is the one shining region left until the far side of the grave . . . O Rome, how I love to return to your deceptions, how eagerly I run over day by day the time when I was intoxicated with you![30]

'Home' is not a physical place but a mobile need; wherever one is, home is always to be found somewhere else. As Herzen's life unfolds in England, a sunless land of overly practical if kindly people, the home he needs will change countries, from a place of snow to sun, from the intimate village outside Moscow to the languid cafés of Rome. Herzen will always have a home, so long as he can change how it looks. This ironic, slightly bitter, knowledge about his need for 'home' came to Herzen as an older man; he acknowledged that he would never feel complete. Finally he came to terms with insufficiency; it is permanent, the scar does not heal. And this same power of displacing 'home' was what he hoped for others who did not pack their bags when the borders opened in March of 1848, who did not return to the loved world of their childhood, their language, their soil.

I have perhaps unfairly modulated Herzen's voice, which is that of a man who is more curious than censorious; as a writer he understood that moral 'points' are best left implicit in the stories of individual lives. Yet if I have done him this injustice, it is only because in his pages detailing the disastrous schemes of émigré bankers, the rage of Serbian poets reading nearly accurate English translations of their work, the fight of many political émigrés to prevent the dissolution of socialist ideals in the acid of Slavic pseudo-religiosity – that these portraits of foreigners struggling to create a life abroad which yet does not cut them off from the past seem emblematic lives, just as the assertions of nationalism which took form in the last century are emblematic of the dangers of other assertions of racial, sexual or religious identity.

In modern society, anthropology has become a threat to liberty. Anthropological man or anthropological woman withdraws from the impurities and difficulties of experiencing *difference*. His or her *nomos* is racial solidarity, ethnicity, sexual practice, age – an entire society of self-referential identities. But the foreigner conscious of the very fact of foreignness cannot so easily withdraw. He or she has to salvage, if possible, something from the very voyage out. The words of Daniel Stern in observing the foreigners around her reluctant to leave Paris might be conceived as this imperative: 'Look in the mirror and see someone else.'

Like Manet, Herzen sought to understand displacement not as something gone wrong, but as a process which had its own form and possibility. In particular Herzen saw that his displacement from Russia had created a new kind of freedom in his life, a freedom of self apart from place, a freedom he felt strongly, but felt to be so new, so modern, that he could not claim to define it. Indeed, that very inability to say neatly and precisely who he was added to his sense of freedom. In this, he became the first, the emblematic, and in the very qualities of his introspection and questioning of his condition, perhaps the greatest of foreigners.

In a way it is always a temptation for individuals who are displaced to idealize their roots as solid and secure, to make still photographs of the past while the present unfolds like a film composed of abruptly shifting scenes. It was no accident that the passion of nationalism that swept through Europe in 1848 took such an anthropological form. This year marked a turning point in which large numbers of people were beginning to feel the unsettling effects of industrialism and rapid urban migration. The overt targets of the national upheavals were the dynasties of the *ancien regime*: the Habsburgs, (especially its cadet branch in the House of Savoy), the Hohenlohes, the Hohenzollern and Hohenstaufen penetration of the Russian aristocracy. But those who took aim at the past in 1848 were people disturbed by a present whose terrors they could feel but not clearly name. The Italians who rose against the Habsburgs were northerners, living in cities like Milano in which significant beginnings of manufacturing had occurred; the Poles, Bohemians and Bavarians who rose against their monarchs lived in places where small farms were, throughout the 1830s and 1840s being closed or incorporated into large estates, lands in which massive numbers of young people were leaving the land. From the onset of mercantile development after 1815, the cities to which immigrants came were less and less places of a settled 'native' population, settled in its position, habits, or domiciles; the imagery of 'native' versus 'foreign' was used by people who were themselves constantly migrating within the nation, 'restless unto death' as Tocqueville described them.

It was under these conditions that the ideal of a national *being* appealed to those who were displaced. Urban migration and its attendant economics was one of the forces which created nationalism, an image of some fixed place necessary for those who were experiencing displacement. 'A world dissolving into chaos': against it the land stands as a measure of the enduring; its being is set against the trials of one's own becoming.

The 'chaos' of economic redeployment and the migration of labour which began in the mid-nineteenth century seems unlikely to abate in a globalizing world. The motives for cultural idealization will be as strong for us, perhaps stronger, than they were for the people who lived through the first great age of industrial capitalism. The era of the 'universal citizen' celebrated by Kant was an era which could not conceive of mass migration, and which imagined capital as comfortably stationary when invested in land and estates. The era of the 'universal citizen' in the eighteenth century which produced constitutional ideas seemingly applicable anywhere – in provincial, self-serious America equally as in the France of a thousand courtesies married to smiling ironies – this era celebrated balance, its social imagination was of equilibrium. In an unbalanced material world, the need arises instead for a being-in-place.

The foreigner is the figure who has to cope with the dangers which lurk in this need. Since the foreigner cannot become a universal citizen, cannot throw off the mantle of nationalism, then the only way he or she can cope with the heavy baggage of culture is to subject it to certain kinds of displacement, which lighten its burdensome weight. And in this effort to displace the imagery of culture and folkways the foreigner is engaged in a work akin to that of the modern artist whose energies have, in the last century, been marshalled not so much to represent objects as to displace them.

The Cracking of *The Large Glass*

I began this essay with a work of art and I should like to end it with one. In 1926 *The Large Glass* of Marcel Duchamp was broken after being shown for the first time in public, at the Brooklyn Museum in New York. Accounts of what happened vary; some say a workman dropped this construction in glass by accident, others claim a janitor thought it was a piece of junk and pitched it into a garbage bin. Whatever the means the result was surprising; the cracked panes of glass seemed appropriate additions to the wire, dust, aluminum foil and paint attached to the structure. Indeed, the cracking of the glass panes seemed to give a new importance to these elements painted, pasted or dusted on them.

Duchamp's great passion was chess; he was a member of the French Olympic Chess team in 1928, and the devisor of several innovative endgame gambits. This same strategic passion is manifest in his visual efforts. In the layer upon layer of clues, references and false starts impregnated upon this construction over the course of ten years, from 1913 to 1923, *The Large Glass* has claim to be the most cerebrally complicated image of our time. If these meanings are obscure – a difficulty compounded by Duchamp's decision in 1923 to leave the piece incomplete – he was, as in a game of chess, constantly engaged in the intentional activity of moving with a reason. The obscure and the incomplete are not the same as the unthinking move which spells death to the professional chess player. The cracking of the medium in which Duchamp made his moves is thus all the more remarkable in its effect of binding the clues together.

The full title of this work is *The Bride Stripped Bare by Her Bachelors*, a title which may suggest that the complicated moves Duchamp is engaged in are erotic as well as optical. By the time Duchamp stopped working on it, *The Large Glass: The Bride Stripped Bare by Her Bachelors* contained an assemblage of malic molds, chocolate grinders, suspension rings, bayonets, neckties, toboggans, scissors, mortice joints and other signs which related the world of the bride in an upper glass panel to the world of the bachelors in the lower (as Duchamp labelled them).

That connection between these two panes of glass in one way would be as familiar to any French child today as in Duchamp's youth. In country fairs in France there is often a booth in which a bride doll is placed surrounded by male suitors, the suitors carved from bowling pins; the person who can knock all these pins down with a light ball made of twine is given the bride doll. In 1916 Duchamp had created a work called *With Hidden Noise* in which just such a ball of twine is enclosed between two brass plates joined by four bolts. Hidden within this ball is a small object which rattles when the ball is shaken, again like the twine ball at the country fairs one uses to knock down the bachelors. At country fairs, as I say, this has always been a popular game, and Duchamp seems to have chosen the title of his own puzzle well, a game of sexual conquest played with the concentration and seriousness people invest in playing other games, and also the same detachment.

The moralizing connection to Manet's *The Bar at the Folies-Bergère* which comes to mind is not perhaps as important as the relation between the use of a mirror in Manet's painting and the use of glass in Duchamp's construction. We know well enough from Duchamp himself what he intended by the use of glass. Duchamp sought to challenge 'the usual sensory evidence enabling one to have an ordinary perception of an object'.[31] By using glass, he could instead establish the character of objects in ways that subvert this retinal understanding; objects no longer exist as physical experiences, since the eye could look behind them, through clear glass; the glass took away from their substantiality. Within the reality established by glass, one would instead understand, 'from the point of view of mass, a plane (generating the object's form by means of elementary parallelism) composed of elements of light'.[32] Put another way, the use of glass was Duchamp's way to help the mind 'see' – in the sense we have when we speak of a mental act in terms of 'I see what you mean' – apart from dependence upon what the eye sees.

Glass was thus the medium through which Duchamp sought to gain power over the physical world, to break the dependence of the mind upon the information provided by the retina. And the breaking of the glass in 1926 was suddenly to reveal that he could not take power over the physical world in this way. The revelation was not exactly the dispelling of an illusion, but rather the physical thing reclaimed from Duchamp, the cracks and splints of glass reclaiming the reality of sensate experience beyond the stratagems of the maker. In the same way Manet's mirror recovers the reality of those bottles and fruits on the bar which, seen in themselves, without the work of displacement, are ghost objects of no retinal reality.

To re-envision others and oneself as concrete, particular human beings rather than as cultural types, may also depend upon such unexpected turns: not the destruction of frames of reference but rather something like their cracking. That unexpected turn, that displacement, is what makes it possible for a foreigner to become a Russian somewhere else, and for a work of modern art to become modern.

– Notes –

The Jewish Ghetto in Venice

1 Quoted in Brian Pullan, *Rich and Poor in Renaissance Venice* (Oxford: Blackwell, 1971), p.484.
2 Quoted in Pullan, *Rich and Poor*, p.495.
3 Pullan, *Rich and Poor*, p.486.
4 Quoted in Benjamin Ravid, 'The Establishment of the Ghetti of Venice', in Gaetano Cozzi (ed.), *Gli Ebrei e Venezia* (Milan: Edizioni di Comunita, 1987), p.215.
5 Ibid.
6 Pietro Aretino, Ragionamenti, quoted and translated in Georgina Masson, *Courtesans of the Italian Renaissance* (New York: St Martin's Press, 1975), p.24.
7 Quoted in Masson, *Courtesans*, p.152.
8 Guido Ruggiero, *The Boundaries of Eros: Sex Crime and Sexuality in Renaissance Venice* (New York: Oxford University Press, 1985), p.9.
9 Benjamin Ravid, op. cit.
10 Masson, *Courtesans*, p.152.
11 cf. Elliott Horowitz, 'Coffee, Coffeehouses, and the Nocturnal Rituals of Early Modern Jewry', *AJS Review* 14 (1988), pp.17–46.
12 Aristotle, *Nichomachean Ethics*, 1258b.
13 Quoted in L. C. Knights, *Drama and Society in the Age of Jonson* (New York: Norton, 1968), p.165.
14 Kenneth R. Stow, 'Sanctity and the Construction of Space: The Roman Ghetto as Sacred Space', in Menachem Mor (ed.), *Jewish Assimilation, Acculturation and Accommodation* (Lanham: Creighton, 1989) p.54.

15 Frederick Lane, *Venice: A Maritime Republic* (Baltimore: Johns Hopkins University Press, 1973), p.147.
16 William Shakespeare, *The Merchant of Venice*, ed. W. M. Merchant (London: Penguin, 1967], III.iii.26–31.
17 Shakespeare, *Merchant of Venice*, IV.i. 215–16.
18 Shakespeare, *Merchant of Venice*, III.i.65ff.
19 Howard Adelman, 'Leon Modena: The Autobiography and the Man', in Mark R. Cohen (ed.), *The Autobiography of a Seventeenth-Century Rabbi: Leon Modena's 'Life of Judah'* (Princeton: Princeton University Press, 1988) p.28; this article contains an excellent biographic supplement to Modena's own autobiography, pp.19–38.
20 Adelman, 'Modena,' p.31.
21 Natalie Z. Davis, 'Fame and Secrecy: Leon Modena's Life as an Early Modern Autobiography', in Cohen (ed.), *The Autobiography of a Seventeenth-Century Venetian Rabbi*, p.68.
22 Leon Modena, 'The Life of Judah', in Cohen, *The Autobiography of a Seventeenth-Century Venetian Rabbi*, p.144.
23 Modena, 'The Life of Judah', p.14.
24 Modena, 'The Life of Judah', p.159.
25 Modena, 'The Life of Judah', p.162.

The Foreigner

1 Charles de Feir, *Guide du Salon de Paris 1882* (Paris, 1882) p.23; for a full list of contemporary criticisms of this painting see T. J. Clark, *The Painting of Modern Life: Paris in the Art of Manet and his Followers* (Princeton: Princeton University Press, 1986) pp. 310–11, fn. 65.
2 Jules Compte, quoted and translated by T. J. Clark, *The Painting of Modern Life*, p.240.

3 Henri Houssaye, 'Le Salon de 1882,' *L'Art francais depuis dix ans* (Paris, 1883), p.242; I have used Clark's translation, though the diction of the French original is much more emphatic; see Clark, *The Painting of Modern Life*, p. 243.
4 Isaiah Berlin, *Vico and Herder: Two Studies in the History of Ideas* (London: The Hogarth Press, 1976), p.xxiii.
5 Berlin, *Vico and Herder*, pp 197–8.
6 Daniel Stern, *Oeuvres*, vol. 6, p.353.
7 Stern, *Oeuvres*, vol. 6.
8 Stern, *Oeuvres*, vol. 6, p.466.
9 Sophocles, *Oedipus the King*, trans. David Greene (Chicago: University of Chicago Press, 1954) p.55; original, *Oedipus Tyraneus*, Loeb: 1030–5.
10 *Oedipus the King*, p.73; *Oedipus Tyraneus*, 1453.
11 In this and the following three sentences I have taken the liberty of quoting myself; these sentences open my book *The Conscience of the Eye* (New York: Knopf, 1991), pp.5–6.
12 Harvey Cox, *The Secular City* (revised edn; New York: Macmillan, 1966), p.49.
13 Translated and quoted in Jaroslav Pelikan, *Jesus through the Centuries* (New Haven: Yale University Press, 1985), pp.49–50.
14 Augustine, *The City of God*, trans. Gerald G. Walsh, S.J., et al. (New York; Image, 1958), p.325.
15 Sophocles, *Oedipus Coloneus* (Cambridge, MA: Loeb Classical Library), 607–20.
16 Herzen, *My Past and Thoughts*, III, p.1024.
17 Ibid.
18 Herzen, *My Past and Thoughts*, III, p.1025.
19 Herzen, *My Past and Thoughts*, III, p.1399.
20 Ibid.
21 It is an insight which may bear on a large study of Mexican immigrants and Mexican-Americans which

found '. . . the higher the level of acculturation (or "Americanization") the greater the prevalence of . . . alcohol and drug abuse or dependance, phobia, and antisocial personality': Alejandro Portes and Ruben Rumbaut, *Immigrant America: A Portrait* (Berkeley, CA.: University of California Press, 1990), p.169.
22 Printed in Herzen, *My Past and Thoughts*, III, p.1418.
23 Herzen, *My Past and Thoughts*, III, p.1065.
24 Portes and Rumbaut, *Immigrant America*, p.141.
25 Herzen, *My Past and Thoughts*, Vol. II, p.686.
26 Herzen, *My Past and Thoughts*, III, p.1386.
27 Herzen, *My Past and Thoughts*, III, p.1397.
28 cf. Sigmund Freud, *New Introductory Lectures on Psychoanalysis*, chk page.
29 An 'off-the-record' remark at the Council on Foreign Relations (but why should it be?).
30 Herzen, *My Past and Thoughts*, II, p.655.
31 Quoted in Gloria Moure, *Marcel Duchamp*, trans. Joanna Martinez (New York: Rizzoli, 1988), p.21.
32 Ibid.

Notting Hill Editions

Notting Hill Editions is devoted to the best in essay writing. Our authors, living and dead, cover a broad range of non-fiction, but all display the virtues of brevity, soul and wit.

Our commitment to reinvigorating the essay as a literary form extends to our website, where we host the wonderful Essay Library, a home for the world's most important and enjoyable essays, including the facility to search, save your favourites and add your comments and suggestions.

To discover more, please visit
www.nottinghilleditions.com

Other titles from Notting Hill Editions*

Smoke
by John Berger & Selçuk Demirel

John Berger joins forces again with Turkish illustrator Selçuk Demirel. This charming pictorial essay reflects on the cultural implications of smoking through a series of brilliantly inventive illustrations.

Wandering Jew: The Search for Joseph Roth
by Dennis Marks

Joseph Roth was one of the most enigmatic writers of the twentieth century. Born in the Habsburg Empire and dying in Paris in 1939, he was a perpetual traveller, a prophet and a compulsive liar. Dennis Marks makes a journey through the eastern borderlands of Europe to uncover the truth about Roth's lost world.

Nairn's Paris
by Ian Nairn. Introduced by Andrew Hussey.

Out of print since 1968, this is a unique guide book from the late, great architectural writer Ian Nairn. Illustrated with the author's snaps of the city, Nairn gives his readers an idiosyncratic portrait of Paris.

CLASSIC COLLECTION

The Classic Collection brings together the finest essayists of the past, introduced by contemporary writers.

Drawn from Life – Selected Essays of Michel de Montaigne
Introduced by Tim Parks

Grumbling at Large – Selected Essays of J. B. Priestley
Introduced by Valerie Grove

*Beautiful and Impossible Things
– Selected Essays of Oscar Wilde*
Introduced by Gyles Brandreth

Words of Fire – Selected Essays of Ahad Ha'am
Introduced by Brian Klug

Essays on the Self – Selected Essays of Virginia Woolf
Introduced by Joanna Kavenna

*All That is Worth Remembering
– Selected Essays of William Hazlitt*
Introduced by Duncan Wu

*All NHE titles are available in the UK, and some titles are available in the rest of the world. For more information, please visit www.nottinghilleditions.com.

A selection of our titles are distributed in the US and Canada by New York Review Books. For more information on available titles, please visit www.nyrb.com.